When Love Is a Lie

Narcissistic Partners & the (Pathological) Relationship Agenda

Zari Ballard

Also by Zari Ballard:

Stop Spinning, Start Breathing
Narcissist Abuse Recovery – Managing the Memories
That Keep Us Addicted

Narcissist Free
A Survival Guide for the No-Contact Break-Up

When Evil Is a Pretty Face
Female Narcissists & the Pathological
Relationship Agenda

ISBN-13: 978-1490407098

ISBN-10: 149040709X

Dedication

To my son Sky:

For your loyalty and patience. You are my inspiration for everything and the most amazing person I know.

I love you!

TABLE OF CONTENTS

A Note to Readers:

In this book, when I refer to narcissists, sociopaths and psychopaths as being of the male gender, it is only for the sake of convenience and because I speak in great detail about my own relationship experience.

Certainly, narcissists and psychopaths do not exist only as boyfriends and husbands. They can, in fact, be male or female and come disguised as wives, girlfriends, mothers, fathers, sisters, brothers, sons, daughters, bosses, and co-workers. Whether the N/P is male or female, all issues from the victim's perspective are equally important and just as distressing as any relationship described on these pages.

That being said, *When Love Is a Lie* is dedicated to any **woman or man** in a committed relationship who is or has been subjected to emotional manipulation by a narcissist or psychopath. Although it's a club to which none of us want to belong, as long as we're here, let's do what we all do best: *try to figure it all out.*

Only this time, we'll do it together…

With hope & sincerity,
Zari

Introduction
The Pretender

The narcissistic partner (N) is quite a conniving character. From the moment he discovers our potential, he begins to target our vulnerabilities, laying the groundwork for his pathological relationship agenda. He reads us like a book and then concocts an agenda game plan from which he will never waiver - even if it takes years. In the beginning, he'll woo and idolize us until he succeeds in getting us all wrapped up. Although he isn't the slightest bit capable of expressing sympathy, empathy, love, or any other type of true human emotion, the N has learned to *mimic* certain emotions to get what he wants. Because his relationship agenda *must* be fulfilled, he will always strive to be the ultimate *pretender* and the best emotional impersonator possible. Emotions, to a narcissist, sociopath, or psychopath, are, after all, a means to an end.

To the pathologically weary N, the outside world is filled to the brim with (sigh) emotional fools that he must unfortunately tolerate…boring "love" people who always strive to do the right thing. The fact that he must tolerate these fools in order to generate narcissistic supply is terribly annoying (to say the least) but he overlooks this because the rewards are plenty. If tolerating is the key to winning the prize and fulfilling his agenda…well, the N will tolerate, use, abuse, impersonate, and pretend until the end of time. He may not *have* emotions but he certainly *understands* them. After all, to become the perfect pretender that he is, the narcissist has had to hone his people-reading skills his entire life, thus ensuring his uncanny ability to turn unsuspecting humans into narcissistic supply. My ex-N bragged many times to me about this particular talent. "I'm really good at reading people…I can figure a person out in five seconds," he'd say with a smirk. And I'd be thinking, "I bet you can, motherfucker, because that's what you *do*."

Once the narcissist has idolized his victim to the point where she's smitten, he then begins the long, drawn out process of devaluing her so that he can eventually discard her in the most hurtful way possible. This "devalue" stage – a stage that can last weeks, months, and even years - is all about control and affirms for the narcissist that he will always win no matter how suspicious his behavior or ridiculous his story. It is during this time that the N typically uses his favorite narcissistic weapon – the silent treatment - to manipulate his partner's reality and get the most emotional bang for his buck. If he excels at this stage of the game, the N is guaranteed plenty of leisurely free time for harnessing new sources of supply, thus ensuring he never goes without.

To begin devaluing his partner, a narcissist or sociopath starts to cheat (if he hasn't already), deliberately lies about *everything* (even if the truth is a better story), subjects her to silent treatments and other passive-aggressive punishments (for no apparent reason), and generally treats her like shit. To the victim, this sudden change in behavior is shocking and she'll usually succumb to the control fairly quickly so as not to make waves. She may become frantic trying to figure it all out, apologizing for the sole purpose of apologizing even though she hasn't the slightest clue what happened. The N, in turn, will blow hot and cold, adding to her confusion and desperation. When he's not ignoring her completely, the N creates chaos on a daily basis for the sole purpose of keeping his partner off-balance and in a heightened state of anxiety. It's the pattern of behaviors on both sides that gives the pathological narcissist an ongoing thrill, making him feel alive, in charge, and unstoppable. His partner's instability and pain *turns him on.*

Keep in mind that these three stages - idolize, devalue, and the eventual discard – will repeat in succession continually throughout the course of any relationship with a narcissist. In other words, he'll charm you (idolize), then he'll demoralize you (devalue), and then he'll dump you (discard). And when he returns (because they always do) and you allow him back in, the vicious cycle of emotional abuse starts once again with the next discard *always* more painful than the one before.

Suffering emotional abuse at the hands of a partner with a **narcissistic personality disorder** can be indescribable for the victim and hard for those on the outside looking in to understand. Typically pathological liars, always chronic cheaters, and entirely void of conscience and empathy, partners who have this type of personality have a specific modus operandi - a deviant **relationship agenda** - that is only satisfied by the suffering of others. Victims are seduced, discarded, and then seduced again... over and over and over... in a vicious cycle of abuse that never ends because, for a narcissist, it never gets old. And, as the narcissist intends, each victim typically develops a codependency to the madness trying to figure it all out - and around and around it goes. For me, the pattern of "seduce-and-discard" repeated like clockwork hundreds of times for 12 long years. Somewhere in the seventh year, I finally bridged a connection between narcissism and the N's behaviors and I *still* stayed, hoping I was wrong and this could all be fixed. Hmmm...how'd that work out for me?

Understand that my purpose in writing this book is not to tell you my sad tale (although you'll hear plenty about it) because *you, me, all of us,* we know the drill. However, because we're not talking serial killers here...because, as the ultimate pretenders, narcissists and sociopaths can and will seek us out under normal situations, I thought it beneficial to share the scenario of my fairly typical narcissistic hell. In doing this, I'll be providing you the tools for recognizing not only the key points of narcissistic behavior but also the characteristics of your own codependency to the whole bloody nightmare. I'll also present you with a new set of reasons for *breaking free* from the narcissist - reasons *aside* from the fact that the N is abusive (because, as we know, *that* reason never seems to be enough). I call these reasons "undeniable truths" because, for me, they represent the upper echelon of standards that represent true human-to-human goodness.

By coming to understand and accept these new reasons, you will find, as I did, that the separation anxiety and heartache that comes from leaving – or being left by – a person who doesn't and *can never* live up to these standards is *much easier to bear.* This is the way it worked for me and I feel confident it can work this way for you as well.

So, prepare to enter the world of narcissists and sociopaths ....the stomping ground for all of life's evil pretenders...a place where names of offenders are interchangeable, misery is never without company, and the clock is ticking to save the rest of your life.

Chapter I
Something Wicked

They lie even when the truth is a better story. Now, I don't know exactly where I read that line - or if it even referred to narcissism - but I never forgot it. To me, it so perfectly describes the wickedness of the narcissistic mentality....the chilling way that *everything* about *anything* a narcissist says or does is based on a lie. Whether a narcissist lies by making things up or by leaving things out is inconsequential because he (or she) is *always* up to no good and keeping secrets is a priority. Oh yes, and there are *always* secrets...so many, in fact, that a narcissist will tell a lie even if the truth is a better story...even if the truth would keep him out of trouble or dissuade our suspicions. Some believe this happens because the narcissist actually believes the lie but I disagree. I think that a narcissist lies all the time because it's an easy way to emotionally devastate the recipient and because lying allows the narcissist/sociopath to recreate himself on the fly, thus creating an environment where he can always be giving himself props for *getting away* with something. After all, to a narcissist, lies - just like emotions - are a means to an end as well.

It is the outright wickedness of the pathological narcissist that is truly mind-boggling and if I thought, by writing this book, that I could cathartically cleanse myself of the bafflement, I was only partly right. Accepting the fact that everything that *appeared* to be true in a relationship was, in fact, a complete and utter fabrication, a figment of our imagination, and a *waste of precious time that we can never get recoup* is a hard pill to swallow. Our love, in fact, was a lie.

In my relationship, the length of time from the N's return after a silent treatment to the point where he would, once again, begin ramping up the chaos in preparation to go silent again gradually grew shorter and shorter. To my ex, the periodic moments of normalcy/calmness in our relationship would instantly trigger warning bells in his twisted head. *Uh-oh, I think we're getting along here. Fuck that. I'll show her!* I came to understand that any time we shared having great sex and camaraderie did not come without a price. Inevitably, at the tail-end of a calm afternoon or evening - and only after he was certain I'd dropped my guard and completely relaxed - he'd find some insane way to cripple me on his way out. For me, just the *anticipation* of the axe falling would cause me tremendous anxiety. It became impossible for me to relish in the moment and I let him know it. "How can I relax when I *know* what's going to happen here....when I can predict your next move?" I'd ask him, hoping for a sign...a comforting word...that this time, perhaps, would be different. It never happened. Instead, his response, true to form, was always to *gaslight* me...to minimize the truth of my words...to make me believe I was losing my mind. "Why do you have to be so fucking negative?" he'd say. "All you do is bring up the past. You're delusional and I'm getting tired of all of it." And then, of course, he'd proceed to prove me right anyway *every time*. Days later, when I'd try to talk about it, calmly laying out the facts and trying logically to convince him that it was his repeated behaviors that enabled my ability to predict, he'd look at me like he didn't have the slightest idea *what* I was talking about.

So, to me, it only stands to reason that the behaviors of the manipulative, pathological, and passive-aggressive narcissist would continue to drive us batty, throwing us into crazy, repetitive "ground-hog day" cycles of digging and searching and analyzing and ruminating - over and over and over - for answers that simply aren't there. Our reactions to these human anomalies are *natural*. The fact is that even the most unremarkable, commonplace narcissist will continue to lie and abuse *because it's simply what he does*. Amazingly, I've come to realize that there doesn't have to be a damn thing special about these guys to make them what they are. Intellects, occupations, nationalities, and ages may vary across the board but the behaviors *worldwide* are exactly the same. So, what normal human being *wouldn't* go nuts trying to figure it all out? Whether this realization makes the reality any easier to bear, I'm not so sure…but it is what it is.

What I can tell you, however, is that over time, by making a conscious effort to change my thought process, I felt things starting to shift in my favor. Now, I never knew exactly how (or even when) things would shift but I would, every once in a while, just know that they *had* because certain frenetic behaviors of mine would simply stop. For example, for a good part of twelve years, whenever subjected to a silent treatment or unexpected dismissal by the narcissist, I would feel compelled to take to the streets in the wee hours of the morning, five-page letter in hand and butterflies in my stomach, hoping to either catch him in the act of *something* or at least connect (albeit by proxy…the letter). Over the years, I must have written nearly a thousand letters to the N – all heart-felt pleas for peace, begging him, in desperation, to change his ways, end the silent treatment, and come back to the fold. Sometimes this tactic worked, sometimes it didn't, but the writing and re-writing, always trying to get the words *just right*, exhausted me every time. *Then* would come the drive across town and the nerve-wracking moments of tip-toeing to the apartment door to attach the letter, my heart pounding out of my chest. Sometimes he'd be home, sometimes he'd be out, but it mattered not because the anxiety was the same. Minutes later, as I made my way home, then and only then, did I feel the huge wave of relief that made it all worthwhile....the feeling that I'd *connected* and that perhaps he'd respond and the silence would end. Up *until* that point, I'd feel absolutely *consumed.*

In retrospect, of course, I see that my behaviors were crazy-making. Fueled by narcissistic manipulation, these late night rituals of writing and driving became my defining purpose in the relationship. *His* defining purpose was to create the chaos that he knew compelled me to behave that way. And around and around it went. The crazier he could make me, the better he felt about us, about himself, and about his entire existence. All I ever felt was crazy.

Then, one night, on my way out the door with letter and keys in hand, I felt a sudden and unexpected shifting in my mindset....kind of like an earthquake shaking loose the petrified pieces of my common sense. For the first time in years, I looked at the clock, thought about how tired I felt, how late I'd get back, and about all of the anxiety-filled miles between my front door and his....and simply didn't go. My heart-heavy weariness and my common sense *finally became bigger* than the urge to chase the N and participate in the game. I knew, in that split second, that my nightly ritual of driving across town in the middle of the night during a silent treatment was over...that at least my participation in *that* part of the manipulation game had ended. *My God, what would I do with all my free time? Sleep, maybe?* Somehow, by the grace of God, I had been granted a semblance of control within the chaos and I relaxed that night for the first time in years.

Normally a fairly sensible person, I had begun to feel, as the years passed, a slipping away of my own ability to respond appropriately to the N's hurtful behaviors. It was as if my abilities to either stand up for myself or to detach when necessary were being very methodically "conditioned away" by the N himself. Questionable as that may sound to some, those of you who've experienced this type of manipulation will know *exactly* what I'm talking about. It was the N's *intention* for me to leave endless voice mails and to cry and write letters and drive around at all hours when he disappeared. If, at any given time, he was feeling *particularly* evil or planned to be with another source of narcissistic supply for longer than a week, he would even opt to change his cell number, ramping up my insanity even further. He changed his cell number so many times during one three-year stretch that I became confused as to which number he *did* have when we were back together. Eventually, just like the urge to write and drive, the urge I always felt to call him, leaving voice mail after frantic voice mail, demanding answers or begging him to snap out of it disappeared as well with that mysterious mental shift. And, again, it was an amazing relief.

Throughout all of the madness, the N became very adept at strategically controlling any given situation. Cleverly passive-aggressive, his behaviors made me doubt my confidence and my own stability and, thus, ensured both of his own. To be clear, a narcissist doesn't typically sit down with a pen and paper and write out his narcissistic plan step by step. He just *does* it, learning himself, over time, what works and what doesn't and just how far he can push the envelope. So when, little by little, I'd stop participating in parts the game, he'd instinctively know something was up and invariably end his silence early, pressing down on the proverbial relationship reset button (that only narcissists have, by the way) and reappearing at my doorstep without a logical explanation in sight. And I always took him back. I was determined, in my own mind, to see it through...to figure out, once and for all, if the dysfunction in our relationship was, in fact, *my* doing (as he adamantly wanted me to believe). If that were true, and it was my behavior that made him suddenly disappear, then the rattling loose of my common sense and my new disinterest in N-stalking rituals would certainly change things, right? Surely, if I just let things be, everything would calm down and perhaps get back to "normal". Hell, I was all for *that.* I mean, he couldn't possibly *want* the chaos, could he?

Then, one day, as I was driving him into town, the N made a comment that gave me my first profound "a-ha" moment in the relationship. This happened during a particularly secretive time where even his place of residence was a mystery so, to the N, my new non-confrontational demeanor was highly unusual and maybe even suspicious. Somewhere during the one-sided conversation on the drive in, he suddenly defiantly announced that it was obvious *I didn't love him the same way that I used to* and that he was fairly certain *I wouldn't love him like that again.* At that moment, I was completely confused. What did he mean, *like that?* Like *what?* I was missing his point and I said so. Frustrated, he waited until we came to a red light and then he simply opened the door and got out, leaving me sitting there dumbfounded. But I didn't go after him. Instead, I flipped a u-turn and headed back home quietly pissed. He thought I didn't *love him? Me? Didn't he see how hard I was trying?* Halfway there, it suddenly occurred to me that, to Wayne, it was all about the behaviors *I didn't do anymore* that indicated to him my lack of love. Son-of-a-bitch! As if a floodlight had kicked on, I immediately understood. He *wanted* me to love him *like that* – to be crazy and jealous and out of my fucking mind. He *liked it* like that. Without the chaos, he simply wasn't that interested. The more I suffered, *the more he knew I really cared!* It was my first "a-ha" moment in the relationship and it propelled me to shift even faster.

As you read through the coming chapters, I hope that, at the very least, you will feel a *shift*....a change in your vision....a nudge in the right direction. You'll "get it" because you're smart and beautiful and you are here searching for help and for answers. I know how it is and everything about this type of relationship is complicated – from the manipulation to the methods of his control to your feelings about him, yourself, and your life....nothing about it is an easy resolve. For me, I had so much time and emotion invested in the mess that, even as horrid as it was, I didn't *want* to give up. I know now, of course, that ending the torment *years* earlier (or at least after making my discovery) would have salvaged a good part of my forties. But I just couldn't do it. I *wanted* to love him unconditionally no matter what dark secrets he had. I wanted to find out the truth and I then I wanted to fix it. So, I stayed. And after I found out the truth, I *still* stayed, hoping that somehow he'd prove me wrong.

If you're reading this book on the brink of discovery...well, brace for impact because the information and personal experiences I share here will confirm your suspicions. Since I'm neither a doctor nor a psychologist (and I don't pretend to be), I can only describe for you my experiences and all that I have learned. I understand full well that a relationship involving a narcissistic partner is very, very different than even the most dysfunctional of "normal" relationships. Because of those differences, outsiders looking in on your situation are never going to understand the level of betrayal. People assume you lay all the blame on the narcissist and take no accountability for your own behaviors and this simply isn't true. In fact, most of us started blaming ourselves long before we even started to question the narcissist. Accountability is actually part of the reason we stay. The last thing that we'd ever want to become in our relationship is a quitter! But the fact is that there are going to be people – and even those who are close to us – that believe that quitting is the only thing we should be doing. Oh if it were only that easy!

For me, it's become quite easy to pinpoint those readers who haven't actually experienced an involvement with a narcissist but are reading my books for reasons unrelated. Invariably, they will leave reviews or comments stating that I'm nothing more than a bitter girlfriend or that I pander to whiners and that anyone who stays in a relationship such as I describe needs professional help. Even if they keep their thoughts to themselves, we have to assume that this will be typical of what others are thinking and we have to accept it. How can we possibly expect others to understand what we're going through if we barely understand it ourselves? It's too complex a situation.

But oh boy, when we *do* "get it"…when, in that split second of the "aha" moment, everything clicks and the dots connect…when the *what, why, and how* of the narcissist's agenda comes together in a millisecond....it takes our very breath away and the ground beneath our feet never again feels quite secure. If you haven't had the "aha" moment yet, this book could very be the trigger-pull that makes it happen. If, by chance, I happen to enlighten and/or empower even one reader to make the right decision, I will have more than exceeded my goal for this little book.

So, let us begin...

Chapter II:
The Relationship Agenda

Women (and men) who love narcissists are resilient, multi-tasking individuals. Not only are we babysitters for these motherfuckers, we are usually mothers or fathers, sisters or brothers, daughters or sons, breadwinners, students, homeowners, business owners, professionals, and more at the same time. Like everyone else in the world, our entire existence is about doing whatever we can to survive and, for the most part, we're damn good at it. This is fairly amazing since loving a narcissist is ridiculously time-consuming and obsessive....a feat above and beyond the normal expectations in most types of relationships.

What the N does is deliberately manipulate every possible situation so that he fully dominates our thought process. This, in and of itself, is the most debilitating part of what I have deemed the narcissist's **pathological relationship agenda**. It's incredibly difficult to live our lives when half of our brain is focused on this one individual. We can never quite relax in our own mind because the N is always conjuring up new ways to keep us unbalanced and insecure. This is not only part of his plan, it is the key objective of the relationship agenda...and the narcissist, too, is very good at what *he* does.

The narcissist's relationship agenda is his modus operandi for living. He has no other choice but to satisfy the agenda to the best of his ability or life, as he knows it, would be far from worth living. Now, the nature of this agenda being part of a personality "disorder" does not make it okay, it just makes it what it is. We don't have to accept it or adhere to it or allow the narcissist's determination to fulfill it get in the way of our lives. The fact that we do is my biggest reason for sharing with you the process that mentally set me free.

When it comes to leaving an N, nobody *gets it* that we already *know* what our options are. We can walk away, run away, slam the door, quit the job, stop answering the phone, delete the texts, block his emails....we *know* all that. And most of us even *do* all that. But leaving an N, going No Contact....it's a break-up, clearly, but nothing really severs. For a long time after, if we dare to look over our shoulder, there'll be the narcissist, sticking out his evil fork-shaped tongue, like a lizard to a fly, waiting to eat us alive once again. There's a reason why some victims of this type of abuse *never* fully recover once they *do* break free.

After discovering the meaning of narcissism, I couldn't get enough information on the subject. I was simultaneously sickened and fascinated by the way that everything I read on the topic appeared to have been written for *me*. I looked for excuses to hang on (there were none) and reasons to leave (there were zillions) but one thing was very clear to me throughout and couldn't be denied any longer - a narcissist/sociopath can **never be fixed – not with love, not with therapy, and not with any pill under the sun.** The relationship will never get better because the N *likes it just the way it is.* His plan, his relationship agenda from day one (which is always clear in his mind) is to keep you, as his main yet secondary source of supply, in a perpetual state of heightened anxiety. Yes, that's right…you, as his *main* squeeze, is actually *secondary* in his life to his multiple *primary* sources – that being all of the additional women, men, and extracurricular dalliances he has on the side. Sadly, you are not the most important relationship in his life but rather the relationship that is the *most convenient* because the effort to keep you in the game is so minimal. With all systems in place, the N happily gets what he wants from life which is a big piece of sugary cake and all the time in the world to eat it. Don't ever forget that when you suffer, he wins. Why? Because, according to the narcissist's relationship agenda, *your suffering is the narcissist's reward for a job well done.*

Every narcissist has a relationship agenda and, for the most part, it's *always* pathological – hence, my rather simplistic creation of the term *pathological relationship agenda* which I use to describe (and explain) the **universal** behaviors of narcissists and sociopaths in relationship situations. The rules and requirements of this agenda rarely ever change and, thus, will always dictate to a narcissist the appropriate narcissistic behaviors for any given situation. In my imagination (which, I admit, can be twisted), I envision that baby narcissists spiritually inherit the actual agenda playbook probably *before* birth and that this playbook automatically updates *universally* as these narcissists get older. I also imagine the adult narcissist thumbing through the pages of this playbook on a daily basis, memorizing and devouring the specifics of the agenda's relationship requirements. It's as if each N is predisposed to want to be the best narcissist *ever*….to get the most bang in life (at the expense of others) for his narcissistic buck. Moreover, it appears that success is guaranteed because, honestly, I've never heard of a narcissist who *failed* at being a narcissist. If a narcissist fails, it's because he's not a narcissist.

Whether a narcissist really has a choice in the matter of becoming a narcissist is an entirely different topic for another book at another time. The important thing now is that you understand that, as victims of narcissism, we basically live the same life. By this, I mean that my narcissist is like your narcissist is like her narcissist is like his narcissist. The agenda ideology that empowers a narcissist to live his life in the manner that he does is akin to his/her "religion" and it is, without a doubt, universal. A narcissist, male or female, will basically do the same things, exhibit the same behaviors, say the same words, inflict the same passive-aggressive pain, and follow the same narcissistic patterns all the time, *every* time. If you think I'm exaggerating, I urge you to keep reading. By the third chapter of this book, you'll find yourself wondering if maybe *my* boyfriend was *your* boyfriend. By the end of the book, you'll be *convinced* of it.

Now, to be fair, we have to consider that the astounding similarities between all of our partners certainly can be attributed to clinical factors. According to most medical/psychology books, narcissism is invariably defined as a personality disorder that forms in early childhood from some type of abuse and/or neglect within a parent/child relationship where at least one parent (usually the mother) is a narcissist or sociopath. I believe that most of us have figured this out and, granted, this definition *does* fit most commonplace narcissists to a tee, my ex included. However, what good does knowing this information ever do to alleviate the problem? When backed into a corner, my ex would predictably use the "abused childhood" excuse to the point that, over time, I went from being ridiculously sympathetic to screaming "Get over it!" (and you can surely guess how that worked out for me!). Even now, although I did witness the love/hate between him and his mom, I'm not absolutely convinced that the dynamic of the abuse was even true. It's very possible that an online article clued him in to the excuse – who knows? The N's lack of sincerity about *anything* makes it impossible for us to distinguish between fact and fiction. We can only rely on our gut instincts because this, at least, will never fail us.

The bottom line is that a narcissist is a bad seed, an empty human shell void and incapable of feelings, empathy, conscience and love...an entity that I dare say might be one of God's few but biggest mistakes – *and one that certainly can't be fixed.* With nearly three million predatory male and female narcissists walking the earth, this is truly a scary time for anyone seeking a partner in life. Moreover, since a narcissist's very survival is guaranteed *only* by fulfilling his relationship agenda, he/she will always be seeking out and sucking in an endless influx of **narcissistic supply.** As the partner, you have to understand that the cycle of manipulation will continue until the day he dies or until you die, whichever comes first. This is why, no matter what you do or say or how much you love this person, the situation never gets any better. It simply can't and it never will.

So, with all due respect to medical truisms, the self-serving definition of narcissism as a helpless disorder has no place on these pages. A narcissist partner, however "helpless", is still the enemy and so I've chosen to take a darkly humorous perspective of the individual which I feel is far more deserving. For example, when my son was younger, he and my ex were both very enthusiastic about the movie *The Terminator* (1984) starring Arnold Schwarzenegger (incidentally, one of the biggest narcissists of all time) and therefore we'd all seen it many times. One scene, in particular, always gave me pause because it seemed to describe precisely the mindset of the N. In this scene, the character Kyle (who has come from the past to save the heroine, Sara Conner, from her future demise) is trying desperately to convince Sara that the emotionless killing machine (Arnold) has a rock-solid agenda against her: *You still don't get it, do you? He'll find you! That's* **what he does!** *That's ALL he does! You can't stop him! He'll wade through you, reach down your throat, and pull your fuckin' heart out! He can't be bargained with. He can't be reasoned with. He doesn't feel pity, or remorse, or fear. And he absolutely will not stop, ever, until you are dead!"* Well, that about sums it up.

I understand that *you suspect something* about your relationship. You have a feeling that *something* – even if you can't quite put your finger on it – is very, very wrong. And you're right. The narcissist has a relationship agenda. To fulfill the relationship agenda, a narcissist will stop at nothing. He will cross all boundaries, stomp on your soul, and basically pull the trigger on the normalcy of life until *you* end it. And it is *you* who must end the madness because the narcissist never will.

Let there be no mistake how the enemy will be painted on the coming pages.

Chapter III:
Recognize the Basic Signs

If you suspect that you may be a victim of narcissistic manipulation in your relationship, the behavioral signs listed in this chapter will most likely confirm your fears. As you read through the list, look deep into the descriptions, replaying in your mind the matching behaviors of your partner - the ones that made you scratch your head, question your intuition, question your *sanity* (and *his*), apologize for nothing, scream like a banshee, or say nothing at all to avoid the confrontation. *Those* behaviors.

What complicates the recognition of narcissistic manipulation in a relationship is that the signs, particularly during the first year of a relationship, are deliberately subtle...deliberately passive-aggressive. The unavailable man, psychopath, sociopath, narcissist – again, whatever you want to call him – is a very passive-aggressive individual with the patience of a saint when it comes to controlling others. This is exactly the reason why women

27

don't often figure it all out until well past the point of no return. I was seven years in before I started even *looking* for answers or, for that matter, even knew there might be answers to look for. When my girlfriend Barbie, observing my anguish during the sixth week of yet *another* silent treatment, said "Well, he's obviously got all the time in world to make you suffer", I had my second "a-ha" moment of the relationship and it almost knocked me off my chair.

The list of "behaviors" that follows is the best *basic* list I've found of the emotionally manipulative tactics used by the narcissist abuser. As you read through each description, keep in mind that the N is a Master Manipulator for a reason: *subtlety is his strong point.*

So, are you ready? Let's see how well we resonate with the following list of narcissistic behaviors, attitudes, and relationship expectations:

13 Behaviors of a Narcissistic Partner:

1. The N demands that you tolerate and cater to his every need and always be available when it works for him. He, of course, never has to be available for you - ever. Moreover, if you dare to even *question* his unavailability or show a "negative" emotion towards a manipulative

behavior, you will quickly experience a narcissistic punishment such as a silent treatment (a narcissistic favorite) or a cold shoulder (if you live together) as a reminder of who has control.

2. The N is aware that he's aloof and indifferent and he knows this hurts you. By acting in this manner most of the time (and for no reason), a Narcissist is able to continually test the mental limits of your patience. The partner of a narcissist is always made to feel that something is slightly "off". You find yourself feeling compelled - and eventually obsessed - with finding answers to the unsettling experience of day to day life with a narcissist.

3. The N will jump at the chance to be physically abusive if you allow it because he or she always feels you deserve it. However, because physical abuse – as the narcissist knows – is far too obvious a slip of the narcissistic mask, the N will typically rely on his venomous mouth as the most effective means of inflicting emotional abuse and controlling you.

4. The N will cheat on you numerous times – of that you can be sure. If you catch him, he will dismiss your feelings, threaten to do it again to shut you up, or act as if you are making a big

deal out of nothing. At the same time, he will accuse you of doing the very same thing. This is a distraction maneuver and one of the most hurtful ploys of a narcissist. *However,* because Ns are like children who give themselves away without knowing it, understand that whatever the N is accusing you of is *exactly* what he's up to at that moment in his life. **Turn his ploy into your advantage**.

5. Because a narcissist knows he is emotionally incapable of providing support, sympathy, or empathy, he will use his indifference to your life as a way to keep you unbalanced and confused as to his intentions. *For example, the N appears to be incapable of making plans with you and keeping them.* If you question this, he will act as if he hasn't a clue to what you are talking about. The truth, of course, is that to follow through with future plans involves pleasing another person and, therefore, he wants no part of it.

6. Over time, a narcissist slowly **manages down your expectations** of the relationship by putting forth only the most minimal *efforts* required to maintain his part (See Chapter VII). The N's main motto is **"just enough, just in time"** to keep the farce moving forward and not a bit more. Think about this and you will see how true it is. To *deliberately* expend more effort than needed would indicate some level of

predictability and well-intention on his part and just may "up" your expectations of him. Consequently, it will never happen and you will be punished in some way for pushing it. The N has no intention of filling anyone's expectation but his own.

7. The N is very good, when he needs to be, at *mimicking* the appropriate emotions of normal people to get a desired result or something that he needs. This is how he snagged you to being with and how he is able to attract women to him whenever he needs narcissistic supply. This is also how he is able to make you think all is okay right before a Discard so that his vanishing act confuses and hurts you the most.

8. The N truly believes that his presence is clearly and abundantly sufficient to maintain the loyalty, trust, affection, and respect that he expects from you (his object). Therefore, the narcissist will postpone, withhold, or procrastinate on any continuing, normal efforts that are essential to maintaining any kind of meaningful relationship. Again, this is another way the N manages down our expectations, allowing him to get away with more and more abuse.

9. Even though a narcissist is an excellent pretender, because he lacks a capacity for a committed relationship, he is unable to fake an emotion of love for you for a long period of time. Consequently, he will disappear for long periods of time (invoking the infamous Silent Treatment) and return whenever he's ready, expecting no repercussions for his behavior.

10. A Narcissist is typically in total control of all communications in his primary and secondary relationships. This is necessary because, during certain times that he is up to no good, he will not want certain people to be able to communicate or contact him. *Consequently, he may often have no phone – at least not one that YOU know of – or he will a secret phone or he will change numbers frequently so that you cannot contact him while he is with someone else or so someone else cannot find him while he's with you.* All communication is only when he wants it.

11. Narcissists have no problem performing normal human obligations in the global areas of their lives and with strangers (i.e. areas where his mask is still intact). This is why the N appears to get along with everyone *except* you. The truth is that with *you* (the individual he has already captured), he finds the expenditure of civil

treatment taxing to his mental reserve and not really necessary in the grand scheme of things.

12. Narcissists will never accept blame for anything that happens in a relationship. *They will always blame the other person involved – you, his employers, his parents or siblings, co-workers, ex's, etc.*

13. A narcissist, in a very passive-aggressive way, expects to be the center of attention at all times and have his every wish fulfilled by his partners. With each request that, for whatever reason, you cannot fulfill, the N feels perfectly justified in asking it of someone else – and specifically of someone whom you might feel threatened by. This explains the compulsion you feel to jump through any hoop necessary to please him even if doing so complicates other areas of your life. In the back of your mind, you always feel threatened in some strange – and often unexplainable - way. Believe me when I tell you that your suspicions and gut feelings are spot-on.

Do any of the above narcissistic behaviors sound familiar? When I first discovered this particular list, I felt instantly sick. There it was, in writing, the reality of the N's true feelings for me for over a decade. I should have run right then but, of course, I didn't.

As you read this book, you will likely resonate with my experiences and understand, all too clearly, my utter confusion during the relationship. To those who do, I say it's time to formulate a plan that allows you to escape with your sanity intact. To those who still need convincing – well, buckle up. Together, we will journey down a path of discovery….a path of recognition of all that is evil inside every narcissist partner on the planet. It's time to look at your life, maybe for the first time, outside the realm of a manipulated reality.

Chapter IV:
Settling for Crumbs

I'd been in the grips of a narcissistic relationship for about 7 years when my online investigations into my partner's behaviors suddenly paid off. Finally, after years of agonizing uncertainty, I came upon a website about narcissism saw my life written on its pages. Within seconds, I had my biggest "a-ha" moment of the relationship...and then I promptly threw-up. Of course, shortly thereafter, I should have cut my losses and kissed his ass good-by but, no, sadly I remained in yet another state of self-induced limbo, half in the game and half out, while he went about his cheating ways, pretending to care about any given separation only when it suited him or when his new supply dried up.

I made my initial discovery after stumbling across LoveFraud.com, a sociopath/narcissist recovery website where I would spend hours upon hours reading articles and sifting through the forum conversations of the women and men who visited. It was here that I discovered the meaning of the words "narcissist" and "sociopath" and made the painful connection. Then, six months later, when I couldn't stand being alone with my thoughts for a minute longer, I signed-on to the LoveFraud forum under the alias *luckyzb* and began to write and converse. The post that follows was my very first and I was instantly comforted by a flurry of supportive responses from an amazing circle of virtual friends. Throughout the pages of this book (and indicated by *all italicized paragraphs shaded in grey*), I have sprinkled the actual "conversations" **intact and unedited** from my experience on the LoveFraud forum. To me, the sporadic typos and breathless run-on sentences are representative of the emotional upheaval we were all feeling as we hurried to comfort each other. To edit these posts for the sole purpose of adding them to this book just didn't make sense to me. Hence, everything I share from those heartfelt and often soul-bearing moments will be intact, unedited, and exactly as originally written. Only the names of the responders have been changed to protect their privacy.

As you will soon see, you, me, and all of the women and men who visit these recovery/support forums have walked many miles in the same shoes and, it appears, with the same person. I think you will agree that, on these types of journeys, there's always room for another wise word of advice.

2009 – my first post

After six months of reading the posts of others on this website, and after hours and then days and then weeks of analyzing the last decade of my life, I am finally making my first post. On Valentine's Day of this year, after finding the word "Thief" written in white-out across my front window and a threatening letter taped to my door, I started googling my N's bizarre behavior with phrases like "excuses that don't add up", "something's never quite right", "always trying to figure things out" ...personality traits of my N/S/P and the things that were making me sick day after day. My searches brought me to LF and here I am. After an hour of reading the articles and comments, I was sobbing because suddenly it all made sense.

Now, six months later, I am going on what I feel is my first week of "true" NC. I'd been ignoring knocks on the door and phone calls for almost three weeks when he surprised me in my parking lot last Wed, blocking my car with his car and demanding his broken cell phone back. [Note: before disappearing three weeks earlier, he'd tossed his phone into my car and stole my car stereo face plate after I'd questioned him about something he said that didn't make sense. Rather than tell the truth, he'd made himself phoneless and my stereo useless as my punishment for asking].

Anyway, when he showed up last Wednesday, my heart started pounding. I got the phone and, as I handed it to him, he pulled my expensive car stereo faceplate out from behind his back, remarked that I was a smartass to keep his phone, and smashed it to the ground. Then he drove off, his eyes cold as ice. I knew that his visit had NOTHING to do with that phone (he's switched phones over 30 times in ten years every time I got close to the truth). He's mad that I've been pushing NC and he wanted to exert control and scare me - and he did - but not enough to answer the calls that started immediately after and lasted through Sat morning. I saw that he left lengthy voicemails before the calls abruptly stopped but I deleted them online and never listened. What's the point? But he WILL be back because it's been ten solid years of this bullshit over and over and over and over. And, although he HAS drained me financially over the years of course, money was never the biggest issue. For the most part, he has always worked. Everything my N/S/P did and does is for the simple, sick thrill of hurting me, making me cry, teaching me a lesson,

making me beg, making me apologize (for nothing I did).
The silent treatments (sometimes for weeks), the mysterious
disappearances, the two weeks on/two weeks off rotation
I've been on for the last year, the unanswered questions, the
ruined holidays and birthdays year after year without fail,
the phone numbers, the list - as we all know - goes on and
on.

Once in the throes of this type of relationship, we find ourselves sadly addicted to the *crumbs*. By crumbs, I mean those teeny bits of attention the N tosses our way to suck us back into the game (after a lengthy Discard or Silent Treatment) when the time is right. When the toss takes place, we've typically become so sad and broken by separation anxiety that even the smallest crumb yields many times its weight in relief – an acceptance behavior on our part, by the way, that is perfectly in tune with the Narcissistic Rule of **"Just enough, just in time"** (#4 from the list in Chapter III).

The N's pathetic, phony, and self-serving displays of affection/remorse are *just enough* to relieve his partner's distress (without having to go all out) and *just in time* to suck her back in (before she figures it out and/or comes to her senses). These attention crumbs are so cleverly measured and perfectly timed that the N, in reality, needs to expend little or no energy to work his black magic. This scenario (which repeats countless times throughout the relationship) is the desired end result of an ingenious narcissistic strategy where the N, slowly and methodically over time, **manages down the expectations (MDOE)** of his partner so that a measly crumb of attention is *all that is ever needed to get back the supply*. In Chapter X, this extremely effective method of narcissistic control – perhaps the most powerful in the N's arsenal – is discussed in detail. MDOE is the very foundation on which the N creates his ready-to-go out-of-the-box relationship realities….pathological realities where he can juggle many victims all at once, upping the thrill of the ride…realities based, in large part, on an enormous *false sense of entitlement* that convinces the N that the worlds within his reality *owe him* and that he should be allowed to move around at will and unencumbered, doing whatever he wants, whenever he wants it, and at anyone's expense.

One time, my ex, in the middle of a heated phone call and exasperated by my unwillingness to forgive and forget *something* I discovered or caught him doing just moments before, finally blurted out.. "I just wanna do whatever I want!!!" and promptly hung up. I remember looking at the receiver in my hand, thinking, "Well, *that* was an honest statement." Sad and disappointing, to be sure, but honest nonetheless. And, still, my story of madness continued because it mattered not how much of a blithering asshole he continually proved himself to be. I was bound and determined to love him in that unconditional way of loving him that I was really, really proud of.

Hmmm, how'd that work out for me?

My N filed two Restraining Orders within the last year and then stalked ME. He accepted a summons for me and threw it out, costing me a missed court date 5 months later, a warrant, a night in jail, and $500.00. He becomes violent when I lock my front door - although I rarely know where he is living. He absolutely hates when I don't answer the phone - but his is off more times than it is on. Three weeks ago - quite suddenly and to the surprise of all my friends - I just went NC. Suddenly I didn't care what his excuses were - because I knew they'd be LIES. I didn't care if he said he loved me - because I know he CAN'T. Suddenly I didn't care if he was with someone else - because he'll be bored in 2 days like always. Probably because my son is away on vacation for 2 wks and I'm alone here, today's been a little hairy for me but thankfully not enough to make me do something I'd regret. However, it was obviously enough to *get me to post here - so that's a good thing!*

There have been thousands of red flags over the years in his "truisms" – those things he did say that were actually true (but who would have thought?).Our second week together, after a fight, I remember he looked at me and said, "I could take you or leave you." And he meant it. Looking back, I'm sure that was the beginning of his control because I was a basket case after that. One night in our fourth year, he looked into my eyes and asked very calmly, "Why do you love me? I don't even call you." And about eight months ago, after back-handing me in the car and seeing signs of a black eye, he started crying, "I guess I've always figured I could do whatever I wanted to you and you'd take me back." Boy, wasn't THAT the truth. And, of course, he is the Master of the Silent Treatment – a famous narcissistic ploy that has, over the years, almost been the death of me. But enough is enough. He has taken ten years of my life and I can't possibly give him the NEXT ten.

Even though we know the game and how it ends (and that it *always* ends), we are always willing to play *one more time* if only to feel the "buzz" of the fix and the relief it brings after a separation. It's a cat and mouse game that the N has been playing his whole life. As the relationship progresses, the narcissistic Cat becomes increasingly better at the chase and the loving little Mouse (his partner) becomes easier to catch. We yearn for validation from the N and if *giving in* is how we can get it, we'll take it no matter how fleeting the moment. During the many separations, we will even wait – painfully and patiently - for the game to begin again because we know it will. The N, on the other hand, spends the separation with someone else, going about his other life with no real worries that you will find a better love. He knows full well how he has trained you. He knows you will be there when he returns.

Even if it is *you* who happens to initiate the separation (i.e. No Contact), the potential for a fall is always hanging in the air. For this reason, no contact requires great diligence and discipline and is often very difficult to maintain. Like anything else requiring our focus and concentration, the longer we stay with the plan (and remain true to ourselves), the stronger we will become. The narcissist knows this and, therefore, will seemingly return on the very day that we wake up feeling the strongest.

Keep in mind that each and every time the narcissist reappears to suck you back in, there is – almost *without fail* - another woman/victim now suffering at the other end. Now, *she* waits during the separation, knowing he will return when he is done with *you*. The N is not only a Master of Deceit, he is a Juggler of Relationships. His proficiency as a juggler is so exceptional that years and years can pass without one woman ever meeting the other or even ever being able to confirm the details of his indiscretions. With the N, everything you "know" is on a hunch. Narcissism is a vehicle for leading not just one but *numerous* secret lives. For the victim partner(s), it's agony. For the N, it's just "another day in the life".

Because the N is so good at being an N, when it's our turn in the queue, we almost *never* bump into the characters from his other life. This fact is the very reason for our turning a blind eye to all the nonsense…to our ignoring that nagging feeling that *something* isn't right. **It's far easier to ignore a horrible truth when you don't have to face it every day.** The N keeps everything – and everybody - efficiently separated by changing phone numbers, changing apartments, switching jobs, telling lies, and having stories in place. My N would invariably be working up to five of these separators all at once (either just before or right after a return) and I'd instinctively know that he was in the process of *disappearing* from someone else just like he disappeared from me. Yet, I let it go. The fact that he was doing it – going to all of that effort to blow someone *else* off – provided me a weird sense of relief and quelled the anxiety I felt from knowing what he'd been doing. Sure, I *wanted* to call him on it, demand answers (ten phone numbers in two years?), and get the sordid details so I could torture myself, but simply letting it go was so much easier sometimes. And sometimes, I just didn't have the energy to face a confrontation. And, *all* of the time, I was too afraid he'd leave again. What can I say? The fucker had me trained like a dog.

No matter from what angle you examine a narcissist, sociopath, or psychopath, the view is complicated. Of course, he'll swear up and down that "complicated" is *far* too exaggerated a description and the problem, of course, is *you*. Consequently, when a narcissist scolds us for making mountains out of molehills, it's his attempt, as always, to make us doubt our intuition and the tactic serves him accordingly. During one altercation where I was laying out the facts, my N made the statement, "You're making me out to be complicated and the truth is *I'm just a simple man.*" Even though I laughed out loud, he found his self-description obviously very clever because, from then on, *I'm just a simple man* became his new catch phrase for every argument where he felt he had to defend himself. When I relayed this to my girlfriend Maggie (who

knew him *very* well), she quickly quipped, "Yeah, right –
simple like a Rubik's Cube!" I found this comment to be so
appropriate and so frigging hilarious, I laughed until my
stomach hurt. Honestly, thank God for girlfriends!

*After six months of reading "narcissist recovery" websites,
I started to predict in my mind what he would do, what he
would say, what he REALLY wanted, how it would end
THIS time. It was amazing. I started to say to him, "I'm on
to you - just remember that" and he would throw an
absolute fit and call me crazy!! Oh, he hates when I say
that!! What we DID have was a great sex life - for ten
years. It never faltered - not one time - and THAT, more
than anything, has kept him creeping back. And it has been
THAT that has kept me from NC. Tonight, when I think of
him touching me after all he has done, I am sickened. I
know that MY silent treatment right now is driving him
crazy so he's trying to TOP my silent treatment with his
much bigger, better one. I'm sure that the creepy things he
does in the creepy, secret life he leads are not half as much
fun to do when there is no-one's back to do them behind!
Since he is incapable of love, I know that he hates me no
matter what he says. He is incredibly insecure and will
ALWAYS have the strange numbers in his phone to feed his
ego. There will always be the horrible "lies-by-omission"*

to make me crazy. Recently he said out-of-the-blue, "You're the only one I've ever been with that doesn't bore me. That's why we've been together so long." THAT statement was so telling to me and made me realize the scariest thing - he will never, ever leave. The leaving will have to be up to me. Thank you, everyone on this website! I know that we don't like that we're here but we're all glad we are. I know that if he knocks and I let him in, I'm done - even if it's for one more week. One more week is too long. He is THE LIE. There will never be closure. There will never be answers. It will never get better. And - since he does it all for the thrill of hurting me and the satisfaction of the inevitable D & D - he will never TRULY leave. He WILL be back to do it again and again. And each time, it will be worse.

Chapter V:
The Undeniable Truths

It's time now to get to what I consider to be the heart of this book. In the next two chapters, I'm going to share the deal-breakers, undeniable truths, and mental process that eventually changed my perception of life with the N. It was a process that slowly but surely caused the *shifting* of my behaviors and the lightening of the weight on my shoulders. If you must, re-read these next chapters over and over until the meaning of what I am saying sinks into your very soul. You deserve to know what *is* and what *isn't* worthy of love in this life and how to swiftly make that determination.

It's very possible, when all is said and done, that your undeniable truths will be very different than mine and that's fine. *Just be sure you know what they are.* To give clarity, let me first attempt to generalize a definition of what my undeniable truths represent *to me*.

I view my mental "list" of **undeniable truths** as specific human qualities that (I feel) the person that I love (and who supposedly loves me) *should* have. If committed to these truths (and I am), when I discover that the person I love is *incapable* of having these qualities or perhaps *chooses* not to have them, then I have no choice but to rethink my purpose for being in the relationship. Now, a person – such as a narcissist - can *pretend* to have these qualities, of course, and, for this reason, we have to train ourselves to know the difference. We have to train ourselves to clearly see another person's *integrity of thought*. Without integrity, a person is nothing. Putting the narcissist aside for a moment, how likely is it right now that you would enter into a relationship with someone who you knew for a fact had not an ounce of integrity? Not very likely, I'm sure. So, why does the narcissist continue to get a free pass? We have to keep asking ourselves this question. Integrity in *anyone* is so very important.

The "undeniable truths" that I'm going to share with you are those human qualities that I've realized to be absolutely *necessary* to the type of life that I want for myself and for my son. What constitutes a "truth" as "undeniable" is the level of importance you place upon it in your life. Once you've created your own mental list, there shouldn't be a single argument in the world that would hold up in opposition to any of them. These are truths that *you've* determined that *can't be denied* by anyone. A narcissist, of course, will always try to not only deny but *defy* your truths and deal-breakers simply because he so obviously lacks the human propensity for goodness that the rest of us were born with.

To deliberately stay with someone who is incapable of having *any* of these qualities and who, at some point, has probably even *chosen* not to have them and, in fact, does the *exact opposite* of what we know would make us happy is akin to committing *emotional suicide*. And when we do this over and over (as many of us do), then a good part of our suffering becomes our fault. In other words, we bring it on ourselves. In fact, at the moment that we realize the narcissist is a narcissist and don't run for the hills, *everything* – including *all of the pain from that moment forward* - becomes our fault. We've *always* had the power to make choices based on what we want in life but somehow we allow the ability to slip through the cracks. Wouldn't you rather be accountable in life for all of the *good* things and leave all the credit for pain and sorrow with the N where it fucking belongs? Of course you would. Knowing this, it seems logical that we should always be willing to walk away and, moreover, it should be fucking easy! So, why isn't it?

We must make the conscious decision to choose, from now on, on the side of love. I do believe, my friend, that you are strong enough to do this even if it makes you unhappy for a short time (and I do promise, the time *will* be short). As a human being worthy of true love, the truths that you've deemed as "undeniable" will leave you no choice. So, today, make a list of what is important to you in the game of life. Determining and then focusing on your undeniable truths is a *gigantic step* towards mentally breaking free from the narcissist. This, I can promise you.

Over time, you will begin to feel shifts in your behavior just as I did. Suddenly, you won't obsess or cry for hours. You'll go to sleep or read a book or dye your hair or do whatever you want but I guarantee it won't be a desperation ritual and it *won't be about the N*. It will feel strange, certainly, to be anxiety-free and it may even feel a tad bittersweet but this, too, shall pass. When my N discarded me for the final time, I felt jolted but, for the first time ever, I was *not* devastated and that made a difference. I would never tell you that I haven't felt sad because that is not true. But the sadness....it is simply different. I know in my heart *it has to be this way* if I want to salvage anything out of the next half of my life…if I want to actually have time to create memories for my son that don't include his mother's broken heart. And, yes, that's what I want and a whole lot more.

Once I determined the **undeniable truths** of a good life, it was as if someone else was making the choice *for* me to mentally separate from the madness. It was as if I had no choice in the matter and, therefore, it all happened naturally…but only *after* I had determined what qualities in life (and, thus, in a person I would love) really mattered to me…and, of course, only after I realized that the narcissist could never and would never have *any* of those qualities in his lifetime. You, too, will have these same realizations and I am going to show you how

Chapter VI:
A "No Boundaries" Philosophy

Now, there are two character qualities that I really feel separate the true narcissists from, say, the people in this world that are just assholes. It's important to make this distinction because, in all fairness, everyone, to some degree, has narcissistic qualities (i.e. a level of greed, the need to be "right", the need to win, and so forth). The true narcissist, however, the one that this book is all about, the one that causes us so much pain and suffering, has, among his many character flaws, two uniquely defining qualities that really stand him apart from the rest of functioning society and here they are (in the order of importance):

1) The willingness – without blinking an eye – to cross any and all boundaries to get what they want, to hurt someone else, or both and, 2) the inability and/or unwillingness to co-operate and compromise in life and particularly when it comes to personal relationships.

If you think about it, many of the narcissist's repeat behaviors – the ones that hurt us the most again and again - fit quite nicely (categorically) under either #1 or #2. And, personally, since I've never met, read, or been told about a narcissist that had only *one* of these qualities and not the other, I'd have to say that they go hand in hand with narcissism in general.

So, with that being said, let's talk about the importance of quality #1 in a narcissist's world. *Imagine a world with no rules and you've imagined a narcissist's world.*

I learned early on in my relationship that trying to beat the N at his own game was impossible. Sure, I might have come close here and there but, inevitably, he left me in the dust. You see, in order to meander through life doing *exactly as he pleases*, the N follows a very scary, self-serving **"no boundaries" philosophy**. Simply put, this means that there is nothing – absolutely *nothing* – that a narcissist won't do to come out on top. His goal will always be to remain twelve steps ahead of you and everybody else. This is precisely what makes a narcissist so emotionally dangerous in your life…the fact that there is nothing – *absolutely nothing* – that he will not do to emotionally devastate you.

When Love Is a Lie

If I only had a nickel for each time that I imagined a punishment fitting for the narcissist or a scenario where I'd actually beaten him to the punch at his own game. I'd write letter after threatening letter of how I'd do this or how I'd do that...I'd write and write until I was too tired to write another word or until I couldn't see the paper through my tears. I "threatened" to "out" him, to expose him for what he was ...to his co-workers or to somebody that I knew the narcissist needed for his supply. In the end, though, I did nothing. Most of us, when we get to that point, *would* do nothing. You see, something always prevents us from *crossing that line*.

The narcissist *has no problem crossing that line* and herein lies the difference between the mindset of the narcissist and the mindset of the rest of society and even most of the assholes we meet.

At the end of the day, the sad truth is that all we really want is a phone call or for him to come over, for us to make-up, for it all to be better. Our days and hours become consumed with *reacting* to a narcissistic behavior....to the fact that he deliberately crosses boundaries that wreck us, insult us, degrade us. All that planning and plotting of his demise isn't what we really feel inside. We just want them to reciprocate the love that *we* feel...to please, *please* love us back...but *Lord Almighty* they just can't seem to do that!

And meanwhile, somewhere else far, far away from our personal pity parties...in their own little corners of the world...the narcissists are plotting an evil revenge and have already begun to follow through.

Remember that life, to a narcissist, is actually fairly boring even – and *especially* - when things are going good. So, to make things interesting, he simply ramps up the daily chaos. *Our suffering is his high.* The more we suffer, the higher he gets. Living by a "no boundaries" philosophy means that he can do whatever he wants to keep life interesting. The fact that other people get hurt in the process is just icing on the cake....*the narcissist's reward for a job well done.* And whether he's around or not to *see* us suffer is inconsequential as long as he *knows* we're suffering. Again, it all ties in with the ideology of narcissism and, more specifically, to the narcissists pathological relationship agenda. Manipulation *is* his life and nothing means more to a narcissist than doing whatever he has to do to get whatever it is that he wants. You, as his partner, are nothing more than a means to an end and, believe me, the end is never-ending. The Narcissist is always scheming and scamming and developing chaos in preparation for his next escape. Imagine it like a movie that runs on a continual loop in the background of your life. No matter what you're doing, it just keeps advancing to the next frame...and the next and the next...until the grand, crushing finale at which point the loop simply starts all over. This is why we are always exhausted and so willing to just give in...to let things go. We simply can't keep up with his evilness. What normal person could?

The only reward you are ever guaranteed to receive for living, loving, or sleeping with a narcissist for any length of time is the top spot on his relationship hit list. All this means is that he comes back to you more than he does to the others. He leaves because, well, he just gets bored. Even the N doesn't really know *why* he gets bored; he just knows that he does. And since there's always another source of supply to be found, he just leaves.

As I write this, I'm thinking of a time, about a year or two into the relationship, when the N, after disappearing for almost six weeks, called me at work in response to a heartfelt letter I had mailed him in my grief. After five minutes of friendly chit-chat, he announced happily, "God, it's great to hear your voice. You sound so sexy. I sure missed that. Suddenly it all feels fresh and new. Think I could come over later?" My demur response of "Well, okay, gee...I'd really like that" could just as easily been translated to: *Well, hot damn, Nr. Narcissist – why do you even ask? Get your cute ass right on over here! By the way, where've you been for six weeks? Nope – don't answer that... you know what? I don't even care about that right now...well, actually I really do care ..but just not right this second because right this second, you made all my anxiety go away....and just for that, I'm going to fuck your brains out later ...and all day tomorrow too if you let me .Be sure to call me now! Can't wait to see you! Bye!*

Yup, I let the N run all over me. Shit, all I ever wanted was for both of us to be happy – or at least I *think* that's I wanted. Who knows? In the end, I'm fairly certain that I was playing the game right along with him. How could my wanting him to suffer like I was suffering be the same as my wanting us both to be happy *together*? It just doesn't make any sense. When the only consistent thing about your relationship is that it's always on the verge of ending, it's time to get out. It's a vicious cycle that we certainly get caught up in and sometimes our own thinking can become just as twisted.

Anyway, what we do discover is that at the point of our discard by the N, it matters not how well we've prepared for the end or how many signs we've recognized…the end is always a shock. The objective of a discard, don't forget, is to catch us off-guard…to blind-side us. It's when we suffer the *most* that the N gets the most bang for his buck. And what better way to break a person's heart than by crossing the most personal boundaries possible? The boundaries that no one in their right mind would even *think* of crossing…now *those* are the boundaries that really give the N a good healthy shot of adrenaline!

Crossing boundaries is one part of the relationship agenda where our emotional fragility….our *feelings*…are actually advantageous to the narcissist. When deciding where, when, and how to pull the plug, he truly does take our feelings into consideration - but just not in the way that we'd like. Think about it…by crossing the boundaries that hurt us the most, the N actually gets to *punish* us for having all those feelings that he doesn't get to have. So, let's take a quick look at just a few of the ways in which an N might choose to go "boundary crossing" and potentially mess with your life. Wow, that's an easy one,…let's see, he could:

… degrade you, insult you, embarrass you, tell the world your private thoughts, think of ways to jeopardize your job, make anonymous reports to Child Protective

*Services, file multiple Restraining Orders against you (even if you don't know where he lives), lie to your friends, accuse you of something ridiculous in order to disappear, change his phone number as often a necessary, belittle you in front of strangers, invoke the Silent Treatment without ever telling you why, refuse to answer his door for days, vandalize your car, tell the world you're are a psycho, **lie even when the truth is a better story**......the list goes on and on and, yes, my N perpetrated every single one of those.*

Yes, the narcissist's world is one without boundaries of any kind. When conjuring up ways to destroy you, there's always another line to cross and that's what makes it so much fun! Remember, in the narcissist's world, there are *no rules* except the ones that *you* need to follow. When the end is near and a discard imminent, the N will push forward like a steam engine, picking up speed at a crazy-making pace. You, on the other hand, are typically unaware that such a scheme of unfathomable evil proportions is in the works. Even though you've been crushed a zillion times before, you always imagine that he's reached his peak ....that there couldn't possibly be any more boundaries for him to cross. And he always proves you wrong.

Me:

There are no boundaries the NP will not cross. We can imagine our revenge but his revenge on our revenge will be the unthinkable, the unfathomable. My friends have a saying about my N/P/S: "Just when we think he can't possibly do anything worse to you, he does." Every single time. It is time to STOP our insanity. It is time to ask ourselves if we want to LIVE. It is time to give our ever-so-understanding children a break and begin being the mothers we should have been while we were chasing the N/S/P around, begging him to come back. Not long ago, I started asking myself two questions and my answers bring me to tears every time. The first: "If I died tomorrow, what memories would my son have of me to get him through his life?" My honest answer is that he would remember how much I loved him but also how very sad I was so much of the time. What a horrible, horrible memory to leave for our children – and for what? For nothing. Our children are so resilient and so forgiving. They really just want us to be happy. We owe them that – for the sake of memories. The second question: If I knew I would die tomorrow, how would I feel about how I spent the last ten years of the only life I was given? The answer: Not good, not good at all. And it would be too late. Sorry about the length of this post.

I can't believe I wrote finally after all these months. Thanks for listening. I hope, if I write again, that I will be in the same place that I am tonight. NC one day at a time is all I can hope for.

So, how do we fix this mess? *We start policing our own boundaries, that's how! We act like the National Guard, strap on the guns, and watch for border crossers.* Without the ability to cross borders and breach boundaries, the N loses all of his power. The fun is gone. The thrill goes out the window. Sure, he might leave. In fact, he probably *will* leave. *But our suffering stops.*

Right now, think about the N and make a list of all the boundaries that he crossed, say, in the last few years or months you were together. Did he call your work? Get you fired? Abandon you on the holidays (a narcissistic favorite)? Now, make another list of those boundaries he could have crossed but, for whatever reason, didn't get around to doing it. Were you worried he would confront your parents? Did he threaten to call CPS but never did? Combine these lists and consider these to be your most personal boundaries and ones that are never to breached again or even for the first time. Memorize them and hold onto tight. Start policing your own personal border every day. Protect it with everything you've got. Realize how important a list this truly is for it contains your list of *undeniable truths*. Boundaries, once securely in place, are intended to protect everything strong and everything fragile about you. No one – but *no one* – who could ever be worth loving would even *consider* crossing these delicate lines. Isn't that true? It's a yes or no answer. It's an undeniable truth.

Chapter VII:
Two C's & False Entitlements

The second defining quality of a true narcissist – again, the kind of narcissist that this book is all about – is the inability and/or unwillingness to cooperate and/or compromise in this life with anyone about anything. Now, in writing this book, I might not have even included this particular game point were it not for a book that I borrowed from Barbie that touched upon the importance of *cooperation .....meaning cooperation in marriage, in love, in work, and in everything that we do every day of our lives.*

Here's the deal.....that book struck a chord with me because, in a split second, it put a few things in perspective about our world and, thus, about my life with the N. *Simply put, our world, your world, their world, my world.....it's all about cooperation, baby. All of it.* And if you really, really think about it, it's a fucking amazing concept. To give you a better idea of how it all works (and why the narcissist doesn't "get it"), I'm going to present it in a setting of *mid-*

day traffic anywhere in the world. Now, although it sounds odd, bear with me because it's going to make sense.....

The next time you're stuck bumper to bumper in mid-town traffic at the red light of an intersection, take a good look at the cars lined up to the left, to the right, straight across and right behind you. What do you *really* see happening in every vehicle? And by this, I mean seeing *beyond* the fact that this driver is chatting with a passenger, that driver is listening to the radio, another is talking on a cell phone, and so forth. To grasp my point, practice shifting your focus *past the ordinary* to the much bigger picture and look very closely. Something truly amazing is happening right before your eyes...something that is actually making the entire process of getting from point A to point B work absolutely flawlessly considering we've got a hundred people in fifty or more cars wanting to be anywhere but sitting at that light. *It's called cooperation.*

Everybody sitting at that light – whether they are aware of it or not – is *cooperating*....cooperating with the lights, with the drivers in the cars to the front, left, and right, with the people crossing at the crosswalk, with the weather, with the opening and closing times of stores, with the prices of food and clothes, with the prices of gas......cooperating with the rules that make our lives, for the most part, *livable and organized and safe and free.* We don't necessarily have to *like* the rules but we sure have to *cooperate with them* or else pay the consequences. We *have that choice* and, usually, we all make the right choices because we want to get home safely or go out and play later and we don't want any trouble. And where we can't cooperate, for whatever reason, we're usually willing to compromise – a quality that may even be more *important* than cooperating because it indicates deliberate intent on the part of the compromiser......a *willful* intent, in fact, on *making someone else happy.*

More importantly, I think, is the fact that, at the end of the day, we cooperate with each other because people are basically "good" and we care about our fellow humans....and because hurting someone else or putting ourselves in harm's way is useless to our soul and detrimental to our overall well-being and the well-being of our family and others we love and cherish.

Okay, having said that.......the narcissist just isn't - and never will be - part of this mass consciousness cooperation factor. The narcissist doesn't give a rat's ass about cooperating and compromising unless *you* are doing it relative to something *he* wants.

Since we're clarifying the anti-social ideology that makes a narcissist a narcissist (and not just any run-of-the-mill asshole), let's talk about what it is that makes a narcissist feel that he/she has the right to cross any and all boundaries and to not cooperate or compromise with the rest of world. There is an underlying cause for narcissistic/sociopathic behavior and it's called a *false sense of entitlement.* The N feels that, for whatever reason, the world – and particularly those privileged enough to be in his company – owes him something. Having a false sense of entitlement about anything is akin to having a "no boundaries" philosophy. Again, it all ties in to the narcissistic ideology of doing whatever is desired at any given time at anyone's expense. And make no mistake, when we're judging the character of others, the entitlement factor *is equally important* as whether or not this person is a boundary crosser and whether or not this person is willing to cooperate and compromise. It, too, is a standard of the undeniable truths.

With my N, I can confidently say that he pretty much refused to cooperate with anything and anybody except maybe the Law ...and that was only to ensure that his mask stay intact to the outside world. This was extremely important to him...that everybody *else* think he was a cool guy. Now, there are other narcissists that swing entirely opposite, always getting into trouble or going in and out of jail, but that's because they feel *entitled* to break the law or at least entitled to *get away with it.*

If we think about it, we realize just how often cooperation factors into our relationships and how truly essential it really is. It's has everything to so with the way a household functions, how bills are paid, how marriages work out, and why kids grow up to be good people. As for entitlement, I think it's fair to say that most of us *don't* feel entitled to things unless we feel we've earned it in some way. And while we may not always agree on why someone *else* might feel entitled, I think its also fair to say that most people that we meet who do feel entitled are typically prepared to provide a good reason. A narcissist, on the other hand, *couldn't even begin* to tell you why he feels entitled to something and will get amazingly hostile if you demand an answer.

To test your N's entitlement factor, try this very simple and foolproof experiment. The next time the N does something outrageous or hurtful – something you wouldn't *even think* of doing to another person – make sure to gather your composure and at least ask this: *I'd just like to know why you think you have a right to do that. Can you please answer that?* If you get no response or, more likely, this person begins to walk away, try it this way: *You obviously felt you had a right to do that. Just explain it to me and then you can go.* A true N, having no answer and now becoming pissed at you for asking, will be completely ignoring you at this point. If you have to, follow him out the door and all the way to the car: *All I want is a reason. I won't even argue, I promise. You must have a reason, right? Or you wouldn't have done it. What's the reason?* Now, suffice it to say that certain responses such as "Because you're a fucking bitch" or "Because I hate you, that's why", while not the answers you'd want, do, unfortunately, provide the typical results for this particular experiment. Your partner is a narcissist.

Narcissists are not the least bit interested in explaining their behavior unless, of course, they are blaming their behavior on somebody or everybody else. My N would do things so unfathomable that I'd continually ask myself, *"My God...why the hell would he do that?"* The truth is that, to normal people, certain behaviors, aside from being hurtful, are so downright mind-boggling that it's often easier just to let things pass rather than entertain the thought that there was *actually a reason behind it.* But in letting things go, we, in essence, enable the N to do whatever he pleases and contribute to own downfall. Whether we can admit to it or not, the fact is that, in these types of relationships, the conditioning process works both ways. It's really a vicious cycle where his passive-aggressive abuse and our codependency to the nonsense work as a team and nothing good can come of that!

My N simply refused to cooperate with any agenda that wasn't all about him or where he wasn't going to be a recipient of something beneficial at some point. Sadly, what this meant for me and for my son – especially during times like the holidays…a time of year literally *drenched* in cooperation - was that we were alone…a lot.

For example, in thirteen years, not once - with the exception of Christmas Eve 2009 - did the N ever spend the holidays with us. That year, he happened to be staying with us – albeit temporarily - while he collected cash from the sale of various items and from his full-time job. Except for a few bucks here and there, he honestly felt that I shouldn't expect him to pay anything since he was, in essence, saving for a place of his own. That argument made no sense to me whatsoever and it was a constant source of tension in the apartment as I stressed over bills and he hoarded his cash.

Finally, at around 7am on Christmas morning 2009,

after a week of bickering about money, he couldn't handle it a second longer and began the prelude to an escape. And I recognized it. The prelude came thinly disguised as an distractive argument about his promise to take all three of us out to Christmas dinner – plans we had made months earlier. He was slowly backing out of his promise but I wasn't buying into it. I knew the argument was based on something else and I knew he was leaving. He taunted and yelled and stomped around the apartment until I was in tears and then he stomped and yelled some more. Finally, sickened that a Discard was only minutes away, I snapped, ordering him to get the fuck out and, thus, giving him exactly what he wanted. His tantrum stopped and with the tiniest of a smirk, he turned on his heel, packed his stuff, and get the fuck out he did. That Christmas, he left us without a dime, not a single present except a set of headphones, and not a bite of food in the house. If I'm not mistaken, he left that morning with about $4000.00 in his pocket..

He didn't resurface until well after New Years that year. For all the years prior to that Christmas and then after, through 2012, rather than cooperate or compromise about anything at all, the N would simply vanish around the second week in October and not return again until sometime in the early spring. Cooperating and compromising – at least with me – was *never* an option with Wayne. He left us every year to go be somewhere else and then – God knows why – he would leave wherever he was to come back. And I allowed it.

Then, on October 3rd, 2012, after a relatively calm morning running errands together in my car, he caught me completely off guard. At the time, we had actually enjoyed a few good months together, leading me to believe that the relationship was on an upswing. I'd completely forgot the significance of the holidays being just around the corner.

You see, what Wayne tended to do (and I imagine it was because he'd finally run out of alternative Discard options) was to accuse me of something completely ludicrous, something utterly ridiculous, something that left me dumbfounded....and then he'd simply disappear. His accusation would invariably be *so* ridiculous that after a moment of being speechless, I'd lose my cool, freaking out, because I *knew* it signified the beginning of another end, and I'd call him on it. But this particular time was slightly different.

So, on October 3rd of 2012, after we'd come back from our pleasant drive, had a couple of hours of typically great sex, and he'd already left to go home, he called out-of-the-blue just a short time later. Although I *thought* I heard a strange but familiar twinge in his voice, I chose this time to ignore it, giving him the benefit of the doubt. Then, as I continued to chat happily, he began a conversation that all too familiar:

"You know, it sure took a long time for us to do errands this morning. Why *was* that?" he spoke slowly, guarded (or unsure of himself...of his own stupid story...I'll never know).

Still clueless. "What do you mean? Did it take long? I didn't think we did too badly for time. Why, what happened?"

Silence on the other end. The hair on the back of my neck started to go up. "Wayne, what are you talking about? What are you trying to say?"

"Well.... I videotaped a few things with a little camera in my car while we were gone. I know that you had that boyfriend of yours try to break into my car..."

"What boyfriend? What.....the....fuck?" Then my brain made a connection. "Oh my God. No frigging way. *It's October. You're leaving, aren't you?* You had this fucking planned. You fucking prick. *Oh my God.* Is that all you can come up with? After we had such a nice day? After we just had sex? Thirteen Octobers in a row?...."

He just kept talking right over me..."You can't get out of it.. You are a fucking bitch and I know what you've been up to..."

"No! No! I didn't do anything! You're a monster, Wayne!!! So you're going back to wherever it is that you go on the holidays?? How can you do this? *Don't* do this. What are you talking about? Why can't you just be normal?"

"Zari, you're sick, you know that? Leave me alone or I'll call the cops. And I'm changing my number so fuck you" were his last twisted words to me. And then one of us hung up.

And so it went....crossing boundaries....*crossing that certain line*.......no respect, no loyalty, no cooperation and no compromise. You have to ask yourself: *Can you live the rest of your life with someone who refuses to cooperate with the basics of human kindness and respect?* With someone who is incapable of the smallest compromise even if it means making you happy – and *especially* if it means making you happy? Or your children happy? Or the dog happy? Is there any person on this planet worthy of your love in spite of the fact that he or she lacks the ability or the willingness to cooperate with the peaceful flow of life? It's a yes or no answer. It's an undeniable truth. Once you answer it, there are no other options. Narcissists are non-human. They can't exist in this world in a cooperating fashion with normal people. *They can't cooperate so they must create chaos.* Chaos makes us crazy and it makes us suffer. And since the suffering of others is what makes a narcissist tick, then starving him of that suffering is the *only* way to end the nonsense.

Chapter VIII:
The Power of Projected Chaos

The more you suffer, the more I know you really care...this line from a song by the Offspring is the epitome of the N's mentality towards his primary relationship.

Without chaos, the N has nothing. The more chaos an N creates and projects upon you, the more you suffer. The more that you suffer, the more in control he becomes. The more in control he becomes, the more he's able to manage down your expectations and get away with murder – right before your very eyes if he so chooses.

The victim's reaction to this form of mental abuse – where confusion and chaos is seemingly at every turn - can escalate from mere frustration to psychotic craziness in a very short period of time and this is what the N counts on. Once you, as his victim, have reached a breaking point, the N then finds a variety of ways to use your behavior (which is, of course, a reaction to *his* behavior) against you and for his own benefit. The very fact that you are acting "deranged" makes him feel vibrantly alive! For this very reason, a narcissist will always turn a good day into a bad day, keep you on the edge of your seat, and act erratic and unpredictable.

The narcissist *wants you* in a heightened state of anxiety and uncertainty 24-hours a day. He'll tell you one thing and do another. Normal everyday functions and responsibilities are intolerable to him. He's reliable only when the outcome serves him in some way. When you really, really need him, he'll be nowhere to be found. He'll make plans for next week and then disappear the day before as if the plans were never made. To explain a disappearance or odd behavior, he'll create an illogical story in incredible detail and then dare you to question it. Most of the time, you will be so bewildered at the depth of the lie, that you choose instead to "sort of" believe it. The alternative – to stand up for what you know is true and call him on The Lie – would, of course, guarantee his early departure and a feeling of doom and gloom that you'll do anything to avoid.

Every so often (and usually when he was trying to lure me back), my ex-N would excitedly suggest we see an upcoming concert together. This, of course, would mean *making plans*, something I was completely hesitant to do since I had been let down countless times previously by promises he never kept. So, each time he suggested a date, I naturally seemed reluctant and I hated the fact that I couldn't get excited about *anything*. When I explained my fears about him letting me down *again*, he always acted insulted (as if he would *never* do such a thing) and inevitably I'd give in and make the date.

Without fail, *every single time,* the night of the event or concert would come and go and he'd be nowhere to be found. I'd be sick to my stomach – *again* – at the very fact that I let him lead me on to another disappointment. It was such a show of *deliberate* malice, *deliberate* neglect, that it hurts now to even think about it.

In normal relationships, the goal of one partner is typically to make the other partner feel good. With both working towards this same goal, relationships enjoy a period of peace and security where both partners seemingly blend seamlessly. This type of relationship is conducive to both partners always feeling that the other partner has "their back". **A narcissist *never* has your back.**

The fact that I could never "count on" my N for anything *ever* was – and still is, in retrospect - the most hurtful part of the experience. During one three-year stint when my N worked as a cab driver, I was probably the only person in town that he *wouldn't* give a ride to. One scary night, after stalling on the highway and coasting my car down the nearest exit, I found myself smack dab in the worst possible part of town. Terrified, I called the N who I knew was working. He wouldn't answer his cell. I called again and again. Nothing. Then, I called cab company dispatch and relayed a message to the N and my location. An hour passed. A group of troublemakers had spotted my car and promptly began to circle it, taunting me. I watched in vain as two police vehicles cruised by but never stopped (again, this was a *bad* part of town). Another hour passed. I called the N's phone (he ignored it) and dispatch several more times but couldn't get through. Terrified, I finally dialed a girlfriend who promptly crawled out of bed and drove over 20 miles to rescue me in her pajamas. She would later tell me that the terror in my voice during that call haunted her for days after. As for the N, he would later tell me that he'd been angry at me about something and that's why he never came to get me or picked up his cell. He simply could have cared less about my situation and never once apologized for ignoring my calls of distress.

From then on, in the rare cases that I needed similar assistance or *any* assistance, once in a while the N would come but it was never without fanfare. My friends, however, both male and female, always had my back. That's what friends do. *Lovers are supposed to be our friends.* The N's reaction to others helping me (if I even told him), would range from complete indifference (and probably relief that he hadn't been called) to shock and disappointment that I would call *anyone else* besides him. Moreover, when I attempted to explain my reasoning for not calling him (complete with examples of his neglect), he pretended to not have the slightest idea what I was talking about and accused me of making him look bad.

Does (or did) the partner in your life have your back? Could (or can) you count on him no matter what – even if one of you is angry at the other? Are (or were) you a team? Think about it. Answering "no" to any of those questions….why is that even an option for any of us?

I saw that Henry's response to Ollie's post. He wrote, "So you forgave your husband and understood his way of seeing things? So the N's live in their reality, their disability? We have to accept they are flawed? Don't hold them responsible?" Now, I haven't posted in a few weeks here but I had to respond. Ollie's article made me remember a time when, after having a great night together, my N answered his cell phone (not recognizing the number and thinking it was work) only to sit there in silence while the daughter of the girl he'd cheating on me with drilled him about why he'd blown off her mother. When he hung up, I went berserk, of course, and he had to admit it - there was just no other way to explain the look on his face. What blows me away now thinking about it - and what made Ox's article hit home - was, finally, after an hour of holding his face in his hands (got caught, poor baby) and listening to me sob hysterically, demanding to know "Why? Why! We have such a great sex life! How could you?" his only way to respond was with a helpless shoulder shrug and these telling words: "God, I'm sorry. I just didn't think it was that big a deal." Of course, that would later turn to "Get over it or I'm leaving! Stop whining" but it IS their reality. It IS how they perceive it to be. In his reality, it really WAS no big deal!

To comment on Henry's first response, I, too, had a slight reaction to Ollie's post and felt "okay, so they get a pass for this?" But then it took but 3 minutes for clarity to sink in. It's not about it being a "disability" because, if it was, well, that WOULD be a whole different story. I see it as having to accept that the man you've loved all these years is really a cold-blooded serial killer who sees nothing wrong with his behavior. We certainly don't have to FORGIVE that way of thinking and the only thing we have to ACCEPT - as hard as it is - is that nothing - but NOTHING - will ever change it and, in order to save ourselves, we have got to get out. To me, same thing.

After ten years of hell and confusion and after one solid year of "a-ha" tearful moments tracking his narcissism, I am on my third month of NC. I never thought it would happen, I swear to God, but one day he threw a fit over something and walked out and something in me snapped. I NEVER let him back in (one time he pounded on the door for one solid hour) or picked up the phone (finally blocked all his numbers) or anything. It's made him absolutely crazy but for all the wrong reasons. It is OVER! I can't even remember if I've shed one tear (which is ALL I did for ten years!) since I had the revelation. Don't get me wrong, he's still rearing his ugly head about once a week - either throwing rocks at my window, calling from pay phones to leave messages I NEVER listen to, calling my mother and friends (who hate him, thank God) - but he gets not a single reaction from me or even a glimpse of my face and I just go about my business. Eventually, he'll move on to his next victim. It's just that I was soooo easy, I'm sure! But now I'm FREE!

Now, I realize that entire days go by without me even thinking about him. I don't care who he is with, what he is doing, or if he has a place to live. I don't feel a loss about the last ten years anymore because nothing about it was REAL - it was all a LIE. Therefore, there is absolutely nothing to miss and I am moving forward very peacefully. Life is good without all that intentional chaos and turmoil. For those women out there who know what's up with their P but worry that they'll never let go, you will. Everyone's time finally comes - in an instant! Thank God.

In the narcissist's world, the meaning of "chaos" is broad indeed. In the N's world, chaos can be as loud as a fight or as quiet as a silent treatment with both being equally as devastating to the recipient. Either way, it's a carefully calculated control strategy and it is *intended* to keep you unsteady and vulnerable.

In these types of relationships, everything becomes about the manipulator and to this, the narcissist makes sure. The attention must be on him at all times and whether it's good or bad makes little difference because *it's the attention itself* that makes him feel alive and important. The fact that he can affect another person at such a monstrous level gives a master manipulator an unbelievable feeling of power. He becomes addicted to this power and will do anything and everything to keep you wondering and guessing about what he's doing or not doing. He is always working towards a goal – that being the destruction of his victim's identity and the breaking of her spirit.

Projecting chaos, for an narcissist or sociopath, is often the prelude to a long silent treatment. Keep this fact in your mind whenever your narcissistic partner begins ramping up the abuse. *Everything* - every behavior, every self-serving antic, and every lie - is a means to an end in the mind of a manipulator. When you've reached the perfect level of desperation, the narcissist then falls off the grid, changing his phone number or letting your anguished calls go to voice mail, refusing to answer his door or staying away from home. He appears to literally erase you from his life. For the N, your suffering *is the prize*. Just *knowing* that you hurt when he's away is more exciting to a Narcissist than any time spent with you, believe me.

Chapter IX:
Smoke & Mirrors

With a narcissist, sociopath, or psychopath, one hand is always trying to distract you from what the other hand is doing. Beware of this. The N is always working a magic trick of the darkest kind...a slight of hand, a play of smoke and mirrors. The N is watching your every move very patiently, waiting for a sign (and he knows what they are!) that you've given in to some momentary relief (in hopes that it's not momentary) and completely dropped your guard. To speed up the process, he'll engage you in amazing, mind-blowing sex, express remorse at how he hurt you the last time, go into elaborate detail of how he's a changed man (from the last dismissal), buy you flowers, hold your hand in public, make you laugh, tell you how "different" you are from any girl he has ever met and how he is incapable of staying away, and praise you for the same accomplishments that he used to (and will again) hold against you.

The N will play "love games" similar to the games he played during the love bombing of the Idolize Phase. He'll tell you everything that he knows you need to hear and he'll look into your eyes the entire time. What he's really doing is waiting and watching for the precise moment to drop the axe, pull the trigger, or both. And he's got all the patience in the world. See, the kicker here is that you can be fully aware of what he's doing and choose to keep your guard up and you're still going to lose. At some point, one of two things might happen: 1) you will give in, dropping your guard even slightly, and get the jolt of your life (a Devalue & Discard always bigger than the last) or 2) you will remain strong and stubborn one day too long and the N, whose patience has worn thin, will then use any tone or inflection in your voice as a reason to kick you to the curb (again, a Devalue & Discard always bigger than the last). You see, depending upon how quickly he has to be somewhere else, the N has no problem letting you think you're "winning". He'll gladly play Mr. Nice Guy, take you out to dinner, fuck your brains out, kiss you good-by, say "I'll call you when I get home", and vanish off the face of the earth.

From Ellen:

Dear luckyzb... Hello! I am so glad you posted, I hope you will write again, you are a wonderful writer, so spot on with your observations! This website has really helped me a lot too. The past few days there were some posts on how we have to take care of ourselves and stop hurting ourselves by putting up with this kind of relationship, and it sounds like that is what you are doing, you sound very strong! Be tough! You can do it, you don't have to be sad all the time, I was like that too, and what you said about your son is so true it hit me right in my heart, I cry and cry when I think about all the time I lost with my daughter when she was a teenager and I was just sad and obsessed over some guy. She is married now and lives 3000 miles away from me and the time I threw away on the N/S instead of having fun with her is one of the biggest regrets of my life. You are also right about how they love to have the drama of having more than one person involved with them. When mine moved out because he found a free room somewhere else he said "I'm just going to stay out there, and I'll come back here to see you" and I finally said NO! And I toughed it out and I'm glad I did. He had it all planned out in his mind, but I wouldn't go along with it. Please stay safe, he sounds crazy/angry. Please keep writing!

Me:

Dear Ellen...Thank you so much for your kind response. It wasn't until a year ago that I had an epiphany about my child. He is always so good, so kind, so on-my-side, that I took advantage of that (and so did my N) and just wallowed in my misery over the drama and the chaos and whatever hurtful situation was created. One day, two questions came to me and very slowly my thinking went in a different direction. Then I found this website and it was like an awakening - albeit a sad one - and I knew for the first time that there would be no answers, no closure, no resolve. The only thing I could hope for was relief which could only come from me and no one else and certainly not from him. As for your relationship with your daughter, you must forgive yourself utterly and entirely and be the best long-distance mom there ever was! It is all you can do....but it will be enough. Things have not been entirely our fault because we have been subjected to the Masters of Deceit. That we have come to realize anything at all or come out of it alive is a miracle. You are a wonderful mom. I know what you are feeling but it really is okay.

Again, I'm not saying that a narcissist consciously

does any of this...it's just that *he does it*. The love of trickery is ingrained in his personality just as kindness might be ingrained in the personality of a really good person. Whether or not he enjoys his own personality, who knows? But the fact is that he never ever tries to change it for any length of time. Even when he appears at the door after a lengthy silence, you can bet that he has yet another escape plan in his back pocket. This is why, without fail, a narcissist will leave sooner *this* time than he did the *last* time that he returned out-of-the-blue. We're always so shocked that the narcissist could return so loving and apologetic, making all kinds of future plans with us, and leave again as if he never came back. *How could he do that to me? How could he say all those things to me and then just never call me again? Why didn't he just stay away?*

The narcissist can do this because it's all part of his plan to control how you react to things that happen in the relationship. If he is successful at this stage of the game, you will always be in his queue, waiting and hoping and praying that he will eventually come back. He places a shadow of uncertainty over your head so that confusion becomes your new norm. It's all a magic trick to keep you focused on just one of his hands while his other hand is loading the gun. Do I sound like an alarmist? Maybe. Am I exaggerating? Absolutely not. Certainly, each narcissist has his own unique situation to handle and, thus, will have to adapt accordingly but the underlying "means to an end" is always the same. In the end, the loving victim partner who likely has now become codependent to all this bullshit, sits and waits and she doesn't even know why. Maybe *he* doesn't even know why. Who knows and who cares? The point is that it's happening and it shouldn't be. *Why hasn't he called? Why did he come back only to leave again? Is he fucking out of his mind?* Could be...but then again, it's all smoke and mirrors.

Chapter X:
Managing Down Our Expectations (MDOE)

For you, when the promised call never comes, it will feel as if you've been punched in the stomach. We become confused by the fact that the narcissist returned to *us* and therefore *we* should have been the one in control, right? After all, it appeared in a way that he was actually *begging* you to forgive him. Or did it? Either way, it doesn't matter because any confidence you felt has now vanished as if you'd never felt a thing. In fact, you're now regretting every second of that cocky confidence and wishing you'd been even more forgiving that you obviously were. There's always that possibility that he was going *to stay* attentive and loving but you had to blow it by showing your mistrust. OMG, the *silent treatment* has begun. The anxiety comes over you like a wave. How long will *this* one last - one week, two weeks, forever?? OMG, not the phone number too! What if he changes his number yet *again*, completely cutting you off, making you insane and unable to communicate your apologies? Frantically, you start calling his phone, only to hear it ring and ring and ring until it goes to voice mail. He doesn't call back but – whew! - that's okay because you feel instant relief that at least the phone *is still on*. That's a *good sign*...okay, now you can wait.

As the minutes tick by, the anxiety slowly builds again. You think about all the crazy, wonderful sex you *just had* and you panic. How can he make love to you like that and just walk out only *minutes* later never to return? Another flash of relief as you get *angry* this time but it only lasts a minute before panic ensues. Where *is* he right now? Maybe something happened....yeah, that's it, something happened and he just hasn't had a chance to call. You bargain with your feelings *and* with your logic. Deep down you know it's been two days and he should have called...after all, it only takes a second, right? You know that it has all begun again and that the pain will worsen with each passing day. You feel betrayed, raped, beat up, fooled, stupid. He did it again, that motherfucker. The thought *another* unknown period of time feeling overwhelming anxiety, wondering if he'll return, begging him to talk to you, leaving notes on his car, on his door, sending by mail...makes you crazy. You didn't get the last word! He *always* gets the last word – without fail and every single fucking time! He set you up, he tricked you. And at the same time that you want him to just show up, you wish he would die.

What the narcissist does particularly well and with steadfast precision is use his various behaviors to *manage down our expectations of the relationship (MDOE)* so that we expect less and less and he gets away with more and more. He does this slowly over time with each silent treatment, broken promise, and other disappointing and crazy-making behaviors. For him, the energy expended to get us back must, at some point, become next to nothing or we become *worth* nothing. Do you understand that? MDOE is something that an N starts from almost day one and/or from the first fight forward. He will work this slowly and methodically over many months and years, ensuring that the **crumbs of attention** needed to lure you back to the game are kept as low as they can go. Sure, in the beginning, he may have to fight just a wee bit harder to lure you back in, but the future rewards – when he has successfully managed down your expectations so that he basically has to pull no weight - are well worth this initial inconvenience.

You see, when a "normal" partner *deliberately* expends more effort than needed in *any* part of the relationship, this is usually an indication of healthy predictability and well-intention. In such cases, the other "normal" partner, upon noticing the efforts, will naturally reciprocate and maybe even "up" his or her expectations, thus keeping the momentum going. In a narcissist's world, the N has *no intention* of living up to anyone's expectations (but his own, of course) so continually working to *manage down* the expectations of those around him keeps him from having to work too hard at anything. It's quite a brilliant strategy actually.

Me:

Now, today is a good day. I did feel that twinge today - but only for a second - and then I started writing. I am a writer by trade and I spend many hours of my day writing for others. Today was the first time I actually wrote something that had nothing to do with anything except me. This minute, it feels very good. Tomorrow, I hope the same. Now when I am driving and I start to wonder where he is or what he is doing, I just think, "It doesn't matter where he is or what he is doing because, if he were here with you now, you know EXACTLY what he'd be doing - and it would just be another beginning to another horrible end...until the next time." This always moves me on to another thought. Realizing the fact that there will never be the closure we have been so desperately seeking has changed my level of anxiety. Not that I NEVER have the anxiety - it just exists at a cope-able level.

Six months ago, I couldn't see myself doing NC at all. I'd read about it, know it was the only way, yet never even attempt it. Then, within the past two months, he did one or two things that - believe it or not - I actually found unforgivable (even though they were no worse than any of his other abusive antics) to the point that I could ignore the phone calls and the pounding at the door. It happened without me really thinking about it. Like my time for NC had come. I'm not silly enough to think that I will never see him again. He will surface. My friend said to me yesterday, "Make sure it's over for you because we all know that - as always - it is NOT over for him." So, every day is a work-in-progress.

The sheer number of normal things that the N won't do *for* you or *with* you are quite amazing. Normal responsibilities put him out, cramp his style, and become intolerable. He shirks all obligations to you, his family, and, eventually, to whomever he works for. Nothing is ever his fault – ever. He feels a *false sense of entitlement* every day, all day and there's no convincing him otherwise. He *hates to cooperate and compromise.* In fact, it infuriates him.

Oh yes, mine chooses to live in a hotel (and not a nice one) and complain about the daily rent rather than get an apartment. In fact, he hasn't paid "rent" in over a year. He'd stay at his mom's until she'd demand money and then he'd move on to his dad. When his dad kicked him out, he'd come here and have a pocketful of cash while I struggled to pay the bills. When I finally lost it and demanded money, he'd pack his stuff up and stomp out - after being here months - and move on to whoever happened to be left out of his friends. He fully expected to live for free everywhere since, well, he was "saving" for an apartment. Once in awhile he'd buy something - toilet paper or food - but it was all about him and not helping. Disgusting, selfish behavior no matter how you look at it.

I couldn't believe the audacity of him moving out and immediately paying $40.00/night to a hotel rather than helping me with a couple of bills. Oh yes - like you said - then he'd stay at the hotel or at friends for free and still want to come hang out here! God, I hate him. It's these things that I remember that make me sick to my stomach. Every ugly thing - and every nice thing - they ever did was always part of a bigger plan to benefit their pathetic, self-absorbed lives. Calculation and manipulation - it's simply *what they DO. Thanks, girlfriend! I'm so glad you wrote. I too hope that I keep writing - especially when I am feeling that weird little twinge that always leads to trouble. You have made me feel welcome. We deserve to forgive ourselves. It is the only way forward!*

I cannot tell you how many times I felt blind-sided by a discard or silent treatment. Just when I'd think that there were no boundaries left for him to cross, he'd somehow find another one or simply sideswipe an old one.

Now, upon his return, the first initial days and weeks were always the same – lots of sex, crying (me), and my accusing him of everything I suspected he'd been doing while on vacation from me. The N, in turn, would adamantly offering illogical explanations for his behavior while at the same time working frantically behind the scenes to neatly tidy up the mess he just created by dumping someone else to get back with *me*.

You see, all the suffering that you endured during the narcissist's last discard is *exactly* what another girl somewhere is going through *right now*. In other words, when he comes back to you, it's a good bet that there's someone else getting the silent treatment. In order to return freely, the narcissist has had to completely cut himself off from the other life that he always eventually returns to. The N is *never* alone during a separation although he'll try to tell you differently. It's a blatant, fucking lie and don't you believe it. Chances are that he even *lives* with someone else when he doesn't live/stay with you. I saw the signs *so many times* when my ex would come creeping back. The phone number changes, he finds another apartment, moves on to a new job, stops talking to his family....blah blah blah. In the end, the N becomes nothing if not completely predictable.

Eventually, after a few stressful days, my ex and I would typically pick up right where we left off before he disappeared. Now confident that his worlds wouldn't collide, the N would slowly begin regaining his control and I would settle in for the ride. The N kept me *so busy* worrying about the chaotic events of *each new day* that that there simply wasn't time to focus on where he'd been or who he'd been with. I would automatically place his most recent indiscretions on the back burner. This too, of course, was all part of his plan.

To everyone - I am so grateful to have finally written. Susan said it so well - I have never seen so many amazing, intelligent voices in one place - EVER! It just goes to show how absolutely evil is the core of the N/P/S and how adept they are at their game to have sucked us in. What they do is so illogical, so amazingly deceitful, and so opposite of the truth - we are constantly shaking our head going, "No, it just can't be", trying to figure it out, trying to make sense of the nonsensical, struggling to fill in the blanks of even the smallest story, trying to find the goodness in there SOMEWHERE. Time just passes. We don't want to give up - not YET. We want to believe them - this ONE last time. We keep using "our history together" as an excuse to continue when, in actuality, there isn't any. We figure, "Well, he's here with me now...must be okay." To our credit, since we never really know EVERYTHING about what we feel is "off", we try not to make mountains out of molehills. Unfortunately, they know this and therefore know EXACTLY what they can get away with.

Although Ns are incapable of feeling remorse, they will, invariably, have the uncanny ability to mimic appropriates emotion when they need to. As my relationship with the N moved forward and his mask began to slip, my N was not nearly as good at mimicking emotions as he had been in the early years. Or maybe I was just becoming better and quicker at catching it, who knows? Towards the end, when my N had to feign sadness of some sort, he learned to actually push out tears - albeit only a single tear at a time. No matter how hard he tried, he just couldn't push a tear out of both eyes at the same time – and it gave him away. As the years passed, even his disappearances and reappearances were conducted with less fanfare simply because my heart was too weary. [*NOTE: Many victims of narcissist abuse will tell you that, eventually, they actually come to welcome the Silent Treatments and Discards because it means getting a reprieve from the pain of being in the relationship (even if just for awhile). I, too, experienced this shift and, for me, it was a turning point in my favor – and he hated it.*]

It wasn't easy to start this book but once I got on a roll, I stayed up for almost three days straight. I've been a full-time writer for many, many years but never in my life did the words come so fast and so furiously. There was no stop and start, no lack of things to say, no disorganization like there would normally be in a book's first draft. Nope, it was all smooth sailing on quite a cathartic journey. I knew instinctively that I had better turn this *negative* of the past 13-years into some kind of *positive* for myself and hopefully for others as well. Writing it all down was the only way that I could think of doing it. You, too, can turn your experience into something that will have a positive influence in your life. Think about it along your recovery because your ideas will become your inspiration.

Look, I think we all *know* what we're supposed to be doing. *Of course,* we're supposed to be holding strong with No Contact. No Contact, after all, is the only legal way to rid ourselves of this evil. Eventually, one day - and hopefully before the best years of our lives pass by - I wish for each and every one of us the strength to see it through. That being said, how do we get through the "now" time – a time that can make or break any hope for recovery? I know that for me, along with communicating with others on Lovefraud.com, I wanted to read a book that would explain to me what was happening but from a vantage point much like my own. I wanted to read a book that related to me still being with the N, putting up with his shit, having sex with him, maybe asserting control here and there (and certainly paying for it), getting stronger but not strong enough to cut the ties, not being the best mom I could be and feeling the guilt...all of that...but I could never find a book that talked to me that way. So I decided to write one.

My thought is that you're probably still with the N as you read this and that's okay. At least you're here reading, right? The fact that you're following your intuition to find answers tells me that you've got one foot on the right path (even if the other *is* firmly planted in narcissist-hell). Or perhaps you've gone NC and fallen off the wagon (again). That's okay too. Breaking NC is not the end of the world, it's only the end of NC. The wagon will just sit there until you climb back on - as many of us have over and over.

Breaking NC is only catastrophic each time because, going back in, you already *know* that the Discard the next time around will always be worse than the one you just suffered through. The "knowing" is what truly sucks.

Lying by omission - I hate that the most, I think. Even when I had completed my own investigations and discovered the truth, so much time had passed since "the omission", that I let it go, telling myself, "I'll just keep that discovery in the back of my mind until the perfect moment..." but that gratifying, perfect moment never comes because the N is always one step ahead with yet another unexpected Devalue & Discard (D & D). For me, the only way to get any peace at all (besides the closure that we imagine which will never happen) is to cast the burden, surrender all of it, give it up to a higher power. This has nothing to do with God, really, because everyone's higher power is different.

I started looking into Zen Philosophy years back and it really helped me feel okay about letting go, giving up expectation, and allowing detachment. Easier said than done? OMG, yes. But if we want to move forward, it is the only way. And to Susan... don't give up on trusting. These people are SO genuinely evil that they will NEVER EVER know happiness. And I'm glad! I know it seems like they go on with their merry lives but they don't. It's impossible. It really is. Find comfort in that if you can. For whatever reason - we came into contact with "bad seeds". "Bad seeds" cannot be fixed and they cannot be destroyed. They are what they are. However, they CAN be discarded - just like they do to us - and NC is the way to do it. As scary as it is and as sad as it makes me, I know now this is true.

For many of you reading this, my words are likely addressing *the now* (the center of the knot) that is your chaotic relationship with a narcissist. Having not been sure about this "narcissism thing" and certainly hoping that it didn't apply to you, some of you may have come here seeking validation and confirmation and perhaps you've found it. Understand that even though I don't demand that you leave this person, I am *not*, in any way, condoning or validating the existence of an abusive, relationship *with anyone*. I'm simply trusting that all who come to read my book know in their heart what they're supposed to do and will make the right decision. *After all,* we*'re all grown-ups and it's very clear that NC is the only way to recovery!* So, the truth is that, by telling you my story and sharing experiences, the main message that I have for you is very simple: *it sucks being in it until we can get out of it...and, eventually, we all do need to get out.* My hope is that I can empower you.

So, do I think that I have all the answers? No, but I'm pretty damn close and after reading this book and all of the information out there, you will be as well. To explain how I came to know what I know, I can tell you that by studying my narcissist (the monster and his traits), by observing my reactions and my kid's reactions and the N's reactions to my kid, and by pulling myself out of slumps (and working myself into them), I saw clearly just how far his evil could take him and vice versa. My life had become all about the endless crossing of boundaries, of what I *thought* he was doing, what I *knew* he was doing, how I figured it out, and what I *never* figured out. It became about the cell phone game, the internet game, the dynamic of his own dysfunctional family and supposedly abusive mother, the loss of his father (not to death, but to an illness) after which he became accountable to *no one*, his curiosity about narcissism and increasing fascination with his own disorder, and how he'd use it as an excuse for cheating and lying... the seduce and discard over and over, the Silent

Treatment, how I studied him so hard that I could predict his every move and every lie before it happened, his false sense of entitlement and how living a Lie really does take its toll... how the narcissist will never ever change and *we will never ever win* and how our need to win (and to have closure) is what keeps us here clinging to nothing and wasting our best years...how we must forgive ourselves and *how the hell do we do that...*how do we get frigging *past it...* and how the end of this sad fairytale can only be written by me, by you, by us...not ever by them. Life becomes one long breathless run-on sentence.

Understand that narcissists have no intention of *ever ending this story* and will expend enormous amounts of energy to play it out to their satisfaction. If there's one thing that the agenda requires, it's patience, and the narcissist has plenty of it. He will waste your time until the *end* of times with no remorse, no quilt, and no shame. That, my sisters and brothers, is life as we know it in the belly of the beast.

Chapter XI:
The Beginning

I knew my N for over ten years before he became my boyfriend. We had actually been very good friends, fellow musicians and confidantes and, although he made several half-hearted attempts to seduce me during those years, I only wanted to be friends and that's the way we kept it. When I ran into him again in 2001 at a club where I was singing, I was fresh out of a relationship that I regretted ending and very happy to see him. The N was a breath of fresh air that night, as funny and cute as I remembered him and we flirted and laughed all night long. When the club closed and he asked for a ride home, the seed was planted. That fateful night turned into the beginning of a twelve year emotional roller coaster of manipulation that I just couldn't stop.

There's a reason why women don't immediately recognize the red flags of narcissism and that's because they're well-disguised. Of course, hindsight is 20/20 and when I look back now, I see millions of those flags flapping in the breeze and I see them *clearly*. How about the fact that, at the club that night in 2001, he casually described to me, over drinks, how he'd been dating this girl for six months and he was in the process of "blowing her off" (his words). He described with a slight smirk how she'd been calling now for three days and he'd been ignoring her (i.e. the silent treatment). I didn't have a label for it then but Wayne was smack dab in the middle of a Discard with this woman and, from the few stories that followed, it wasn't the first time that he'd done this to her. And later that night, feeling comfortable enough to have sex with a guy I'd known half my life, I asked if it was safe to be there naked right on the living room couch. *I mean, what if she came by?* But Wayne was adamantly confident that she *would not* be by. For just a second, I considered this an odd response since she'd been trying to reach him but I chose to carry on. Sure enough, she never showed that night or any night thereafter.

How could he have been so confident that she wouldn't at least drive by? Because he had managed down her expectations, that's how. He'd trained her to stay away…filled her with so much anxiety that he knew he was safe from her coming by for at least the first few days of the silent treatment - just like he would train me to behave

112

over the next decade of my life. I never did meet or even run into that woman but I can only be happy for her since she was released after just six months in his clutches. While I'm certain he attempted to contact her at least a few times behind my back in the beginning (and maybe even over the years), on that night in 2001, he saw me, for whatever reason, as a far more lucrative piece of narcissistic supply.

Thanks for the kind words on the post. When I do write here, I always feel so good...nothing is more therapeutic and everyone is SO on the same page... Ollie, I loved your article because it kind of gives us an OUT, a different way to look at it. If their reality IS what it IS, then there is NOTHING to do but leave. We can't kick ourselves over something that simply and absolutely CAN NOT be changed. Once we realize that - I mean REALLY realize that - it becomes suddenly so much easier to go NC.

To Susan who wrote "I loved what you said to the folks who are struggling with trying to get free....It will happen!" It's amazing about the moment when it is FINALLY over, isn't it? I let my N come and go and do what he pleased at the expense of my sanity for ten years and I'm sure - now that I've shut him out, cut him off - he feels completely wronged. He'd disappear, reappear, and find an excuse to leave, come back. For the last year or two I was on the "two weeks on, two weeks off" rotation and I could almost tell you the very moment when he'd knock on the door or call again. I was always torn - I could demand answers, risk an early departure, and just extend the horrific anxiety or I could shut up, pout a little, have good sex, and enjoy an anxiety-free week or so until he - for whatever reason (my time was up!) - he'd have a fit, pack his stuff, and storm out. And then the cycle would begin again.

He ruined every holiday, birthday for me and my son - EVERY SINGLE ONE - for ten years. I could always tell when he was up to something because he'd start accusing me of ridiculous shit out of the blue. I learned - through reading LF and extensive research - to figure out what HE was doing by paying close attention to the things he was accusing ME of (they are really such idiots). The night I discovered LF - and the true meaning of the word narcissist, the signs, symptoms, behaviors - I literally threw up right at my desk. I suddenly knew the awful truth - that it would never end, there was no way to fix ANYTHING, and worst of all, that my gut instincts this entire time were SPOT ON! Throughout the next year, the dynamics of everything he did took on a new meaning and it was like I was writing a case book study in my head. It made me sick. But, even though I knew the truth, I couldn't see the light at the end of the tunnel. I'd cry and cry and feel such despair. It often felt so much worse because I KNEW. I sometimes wished I'd NEVER found my way to the truth. There was less anxiety in really NOT knowing, in just IMAGINING what he was doing and leaving the slight possibility open that maybe he really WASN'T doing it.

Then, about six months into the discovery year and about three months before I went NC, for some reason I started to feel slightly empowered at my knowing the truth. One night, after listening to a bunch of lies, I simple looked at him and calmly said, "You know what - I'm ON to you. You can tell me whatever you want, but I'm ON to you. You just remember that." He threw a FIT! Instead of asking me - like a normal person might - what I meant by that, he just had a tantrum and, of course, left. From then on, whenever he showed back up, would hang for awhile, and then start his antics, I'd always say that - "I'm ON to you" at the appropriate moments and, trust me, it DID shut him up, quiet him down, and stop even HIM from spouting his foolishness. I offered no explanation for it. Sometimes I might say, "You know EXACTLY what that means" and he'd just stare at me with that ridiculous blank, deer-caught-in-the-headlights look he'd get when faced with his own psychotic idiocy. My point is...slowly but surely, I got stronger without even knowing it...until that final day when I let him go once and for all. My son was in the next room that day and he does this great impression of me calmly yelling out from my room this cocky " Buh-BYE-now!" as the N stormed out on what he didn't know was his very last day in THIS girl's reality! Every girl with an N - let your heart not be troubled!!! It's your Divine Right to be happy and, I promise you, that your incredible moment WILL come!

What people who have never been involved with a narcissist fail to understand is that these relationships are *different.* Every other relationship I'd ever been in – including my two marriages – had been "normal" relationships that just didn't work out. Sure, several of these relationships resulted in my heart being broken and long periods of sadness that seemed to never end but that being said, they were still *normal relationships, normal break-ups.* One of the relationships – and perhaps the one that counted the most (up until the N) – ended after four years and I was devastated and remember grieving for months. Today, I'm very good friends with that man. Time had passed and, because the relationship – even with all of its heartache – was otherwise *normal,* he and I are able to be good friends and, interestingly enough, I have only good memories.

From Donna:

Dear luckyzb, thank you so much for your post. It shows that even if it takes time, there is a way out of these entanglements.

My point is that I *know* what is normal and what is not normal when it comes to love. So, why I let myself get sucked up into the evil with the narcissist, I'll *never* know. On that night in 2001, I happened to be singing in the wrong bar at the wrong time and Wayne saw a vulnerable target. Having already been "friends" all those years prior, we instantly became "soul mates". Narcissists are very good at the honeymoon/Idolize phase and the fact that we're all here now is proof of that. For obvious reasons, I call what they do to us during this initial stage as having a *soul mate effect.* For me, it took perhaps just one month for me to see a dark side come out…for him to utter what would become his famous words to me over the course of the next ten years: *"I can take you or leave you".* The first time he said that to me, I should have turned away and never looked back. Instead, I crumbled and cried. He loved my response and from that first time forward, it was manipulation game on!

Chapter XII:
Things Just Don't Add Up

Not long after the Idolize phase begins, the N begins to weave his web of lies and this is where our confusion starts. Often times, the lies are simple enough and/or vague enough so that you don't even question them. Even though his stories don't add up, you can't quite put your finger on the variable. You begin to question yourself, wondering if maybe you're looking too deep for an explanation. The first few times that you do call him on a discrepancy, he's quick to accuse you of not trusting him, of being a jealous girlfriend, of being a nag, and of making much ado about nothing. For awhile, he allows your accusations and questions to accumulate, brushing them off as irritations and making you feel bad for even thinking that way about him. Then, one day, you push just a little too far and he leaves suddenly or storms off, never to return or call. Days go by and now you're confused. You start to stress, playing any and all events that could have caused his disappearance over and over in your head. Unbeknownst to you, this is just the beginning of the very first silent treatment (ST) of your relationship...and it's going to wreck you.

Please. I need help today. It took everything I had just to get to the computer to type this. I've been curled in a fetal position for 4 days and I can't get out of it. I don't know if anyone remembers me but I wrote a few "go girl!" motivational, I-did-it-you-can-do-it, NC-all-the-way posts just a month or so ago - which is all very embarrassing now because I'm completely crippled again as if all those feelings and my epiphany never happened.

I booted my N of ten years out almost three months ago and I was doing great - better than I ever thought I would. He was so evil and so N casebook and I was so great with NC no matter what - nothing he did phased me and I never responded. Hoped he'd disappear. Days would go by that I would hardly think of him - I mean, I felt GOOD! Then, I went on a couple of dates (there is no lack of guys for that) because I thought I was ready. And even though they were good-looking, well-adjusted guys, I went away feeling really empty and just blew them off. Felt myself starting to miss the N although not enough to break NC. That was about two weeks ago. Of course, in my N's psychic evilness, he must have sensed this because a note appeared on my car while it was parked "for sale" at a girlfriend's house in town. The day I found the note, my girlfriend said it had already been there about a week but she hadn't seen me to tell me. I just stuck it in my pocket with really no desire to read it. In fact, it gave me that familiar yucky jolt when I saw it and I felt reaffirmed. At the same moment as I was putting the note in my pocket, he pulls up - for the first time in almost three months. I was still feeling strong, walking around the car fixing things and he was just bouncing around behind me telling me how he missed me and my kid and he "didn't know what had happened" but we had been "his world", blah blah blah. He didn't stay long and I didn't say much but he mouthed the words "call me, please" as he pulled out of the driveway and I got that really sick feeling. Of course, I then proceeded to read the note and it said all kinds of nice things which I didn't believe at all. I even showed the note to a group of people that night that know the N and we ripped it apart. Well, what happened next has led me to writing this post. I fucked up.

My N hit me with a first silent treatment that lasted nearly six weeks. No explanation, no nothing. This was also the first time he changed his cell phone number – something that crushed me. How could he want to discard me *so bad* that he would change his number? We hadn't even have a fight! Then, one day, the N, feeling that I'd been punished enough, would finally answer the door or respond to my endless stream of distraught letters begging for a reason. As for me, I'd feel so relieved that the anxiety of the silence was finally over that I'd let everything go, asking for no explanation whatsoever. I'd feel so relieved, in fact, that I'd be high on life for days after, feeling light as a feather. All he had to do was open the door and every knot in my stomach untied. In retrospect, I can certainly see that I was a good little student right from the get-go. And the N, being held accountable for nothing, just picked up where he left off. And I let him.

The above scenario repeated itself over and over and over for years on end. Preceding a silent treatment, he'd either break his lease or get evicted from his apartment and then move to his mother's home (where I was warned not to look for him). Moving to his mom's house ensured that he'd have a safe place, over the next ten years, where he could juggle his relationships away from me. If, by chance, he was on the "outs" with his mom, he'd move in with me for awhile, taking control of the household and, if he stayed long enough, ruining every holiday and birthday, no matter how hard we tried to accommodate him.

Three days later after seeing him at my girlfriend's house, I suddenly tried to call him - and his cell phone was disconnected (of course - he's the Master of the Cell Phone Game). I became instantly pissed because he had mouthed the words "call me" KNOWING the cell was off. I then proceeded to instigate my own demise. To shorten this, here's the chain of events in the last two weeks since

I found his phone disconnected: - (Wed) I obsess about getting in touch and end up texting his friend about what a creep he was for doing that & messing with my head when I was doing good. I did it because I KNEW it would piss him off and smoke him out. It did. - (Fri) Two days later, his number pops up on caller ID and I don't answer (Playing the game and sick about it but doing it anyway). He calls 10 times in a row ringing my cell then my home phone. When I finally call him back, he doesn't pick up. I call 5 times - he never picks up. I'm losing it. - (Sat) I text his friend again about what the N had done the night before, what a game-player he is and so forth. His friend is not texting back but I know he's relaying the messages. - (Sun) Nothing. I'm freaking out as if I'd never gone NC. I am starting to get depressed. (Mon) He calls. I agree to meet him in a parking lot. We drive around a bit on errands and then I sit and listen to him tell me how wrong he's been and how he - get this - knows he's a narcissist. He has a new little diamond in one ear that I KNOW he didn't buy himself. He wants to try again. He's FORCING tears and I know this but I'm crying to. However, when he wants to come over that night I say no. He's still living at his mom's with no job - bullshit. I want him to come up but I do say no. He cries some more, asks if he can call me later, I say yes - he leaves. And never calls. (Tue, Wed) Nothing. I'm trying to call - phone just rings and rings - just like it would when he would leave it in the car while at my house so I wouldn't know who was calling. I'm sure he's at that girl's house or SOMETHING doing the same. (Thur) He starts power-calling and I don't pick up. He panics and tries to suck up to my son in a phone call and my son is very, very indifferent which freaks him out. When I finally pick up, he acts like I'm making a big deal out of nothing, he loves me, and he's at his mom's and can't talk much - blah blah. I'm not very nice. We hang up. Suddenly he calls - CRYING - that his mom had a stroke and he and his step-father are on the way to hospital & he'll call me back. He never calls and I know it's a lie. (Fri) I call hospitals all over town and his mother was never admitted anywhere. I power call his phone. He doesn't pick up all weekend. I drive by his mom's house clear across town at 4:00am and I think I see his car but I'm not sure. I'm sick to death (mostly at how I am back to square one!) (Sun) I obsess over this girl he cheated on me with over a year ago. I drive by where I THINK her house is. I'm throwing up. I finally send her a letter on Facebook under an anonymous name telling her EVERYTHING, what's he's been up to the past couple of weeks, and MORE. Stuff I knew would be the end to all if and when it did get back to him. If it DID get to him, then I knew he was lying about not seeing her. (Mon - the 22nd) He calls, tells more lies about his mother. He wants to come over. I say no although I agree to meet him Tuesday after work and say I'd call him. (Tue) I'm feeling nervous at work about the Facebook letter because my cell starts ringing earlier than he would normally call. I ignore it, hoping he's not waiting outside when I get home.

What outside observers fail to understand is that when the N isn't being evil, he's typically quite the charmer. The polished, experienced narcissist is very sexy, incredibly witty, unusually smart, and really quite endearing. It must truly cramp his style to have to mimic these types of emotions/qualities but he will do it because the rewards are plenty. To say that there are never good times spent with these creatures would be a lie. Of course there are! In fact, it is these incredible moments that we *cling* to when the downslide begins. And the sex is typically mind-blowing as well – at least it was for me and, of course, it sure seemed that way for him. Over the years, I came to the horrifying realization that he was probably having sex with everyone imaginable and that he could easily do this because it was the only thing he knew how to do well. It was his Ace in the Hole and the perfect narcissistic scam for his pathological agenda. Now, in retrospect, I'm embarrassed at how easily I could be suckered into the façade over and over. My ex had a sexual routine that was *intended* to hook anyone that he fucked. Just like all of the lies and all of the faked emotions, sex, too, was a means to an end... and when I think of it now, it makes me sad... and, yes, it makes me sick.

The roller coaster of emotions is destroying me by at this point. When I get home, my son informs me that my mother (in Colorado - I'm in Tucson) called and the N has been calling her all day long, over and over. Now I KNOW he knows about the letter and what it said. Then I realize that the girl must have read it, confronted him, and he now had to call my mother to embarrass and humiliate me into going away (crossing those boundaries!!!). He powers calls me one more time and I pick up the phone and hang it up. Silence. Now I begin leaving awful messages on his cell about his calling my mom, not mentioning the letter. (Wed)

*I power call him. Nothing but a dreaded silence. (Thur -
Xmas Eve!) I call again - nothing. I do notice a strange
number on the caller ID and when I listen to the message, I
hear a Sheriff informing me that he has court papers to
serve me and if he doesn't hear back from me today he'll be
at my house at 8:00am Monday. I call the number late at
night and the answering service IS for the sheriffs.*

*He went and got an Order of Protection to serve ME on
Xmas Eve!!!!*

*I called all night freaking out and now he has shut his
phone off. That bastard initiated all of this! I was doing
good! I am so sick I could die. It's just me and my son here
and Xmas Eve and this morning, I have been so depressed
and so sick, all curled up in bed. I'm forced now to get an
Order of Protection back on him before I am served
Monday morning. He had done this once before but called
it off when he needed a place to stay that week. I am sick
about the girl, I am sick about him, I am sick I fell for it. I
am sick that he is back in control. Help me! I feel like I will
NEVER get past this. This is worse than any other time. I
just want to call and call and call and call - even though I
know this can never be. I still don't want him here at my
house (he lived here on and off for ten years) and I know
that that had a lot to do with his pull-back. He was looking*

for a way out of his mom's, probably fighting with her, wanting to have sex with me and using that as a pull (it was always great but God! so what!), lies, lies, lies, lies. Then - I exposed him and BANG - he goes to court to serve me on Xmas EVE!! for nothing...........what the hell am I supposed to do now?? He won!!!! I broke NC and ruined my life!! OMG - I know this is a boring story but I am literally crippled, crying for the past two weeks since he showed up at my car and sucked me back in to his warped, twisted reality. I hadn't cried in MONTHS during NC!!!! Now I have to go to the courthouse. God KNOWS what he put on the Order!!!I truly believe he won't stop until I'm dead. And now I'm torn about this girl and how that letter obviously got through somewhere and I hate all of them! Oh enough....I am just ready to lose it. God help me. I've ruined my son's Xmas (even though he has been sooooo good) and my N has won.

Slowly, over time, you will become so consumed with figuring it all out that you will become a master investigator. You will search for hours, sometimes finding something, most of the time finding nothing. My ex was very good at the game. Wayne could, and I'm very sure he did, juggle many relationships along with the one he carried on with me. To him, it was all about disappearing, reappearing, and the scheduling of silent treatments. I see now that he had everything perfectly timed so that he received the biggest rush with the least resistance.

There was a period of about eight months where our relationship, believe it or not, was, literally, two weeks on and two weeks off – to the point that I could predict almost *to the hour* when he'd reappear at the door with a ridiculous story. Sometimes, he'd return with a new cell number as well – a tactic that quickly became his favorite and most efficient way of erasing his tracks from whoever existed at the *other* end of this apparent rotation or, of course, from *me*, depending upon which way he was running. Even the biweekly reunion had a pattern. I'd cry, he'd pretend to care, we'd have sex, I'd cry a little more, he'd ignore it, we'd hang out, and then, before you knew it, two weeks had passed and my time was up! And like a bizarre parallel universe, I'm sure the activities at his next stop played out exactly the same.

The fact that nothing about a narcissist's behavior adds up or makes any sense at all intentionally complicates – and, thus, *postpones* - any ideas we might have about confrontation. At least it did for me which is truly amazing considering the countless man hours I expended *thinking* about confrontation. So, during these eight months of biweekly silences, although I cried a lot (and, undoubtedly, he knew *why* I was crying), I said little about my thoughts. But what we allow, will continue – and it did. Then, one night, my friend Maggie (who knew Wayne very well), listened to me commiserate about the situation for awhile and remarked, "Well, if I didn't know any better, I'd say you were on some sort of rotation." *Uh...I'm sorry, what did you say?* From that moment, I was all about getting a confrontation some how, some way. Sometimes, I think, we need to hear the words come out of someone else's mouth.

Fast forward to Wayne's next return and there we were, casually kicking back in my bedroom/home office (as we'd done a million times before), him at one desk and me at the other desk across the room, together dutifully playing *hope and pretend.* Basically, he'd sit with his back to me, hoping I couldn't see his inappropriate internet shenanigans while I acted busy behind him, pretending that even if I could see, I didn't care. As a couple, this is how we played together for over a decade. The truth, of course, was that I could see *everything* from where I sat and as long as I typed and shuffled loudly, making the appropriate noises, he felt invisible and gave me plenty to look at. This particular night, though, the clock was ticking and I had other things on my mind. I remember staring at the back of his head in silence for a very long time…and then I said it.

"You know, if I didn't know any better, I'd think I was on some sort of rotation".

Bang! That was it. He had an *instant distraction reaction.* Saying nothing, he stood straight up from the desk, pressed his hand to his forehead, grimaced in pain, and stumbled to the bed, feigning a mysterious – and conveniently debilitating - migraine that put him down for the remainder of the day. To myself, I thought, *"Well, fuck…I **am** on a rotation. I'll be damned. There's my confirmation."* I remember watching the performance with anxious confusion, not really knowing what to do. *Should I scream? Throw up? Be relieved?* In the end, I was mostly silent. I may have even walked to the fridge to fetch the poor boy an ice pack. Bottom line was that *now* I knew. More importantly, now I knew that *he* knew that I knew and the jig, no matter what, was definitely up. The rotations stopped immediately although I'm not so stupid as to think that he *never* returned to wherever it was that he went because narcissists always *do* return – if for no other reason than to ensure that his victim never moves on.

Did I think I'd won back then? Who knows and who cares. Like a true co-dependant, I let it go. And like a typical narcissist, he'd gotten away with it.

From Aileen:

Dear luckyzb - breathe girl. I think you will get out of this. Breathe. You need to protect yourself and your son. Okay, you outed him and he has filed a restraining order against you. Now you will do the same, right? That's probably a very good idea. No one knows it was you who wrote the FB letter, right? Don't go offering up that info, k? Can you talk to your mom? Is she an ally? Do you have friends or relatives who you can reach out to in your area? Reach out to them. Unless you need it for work or other reasons, take the battery out of your cell. Seal it in a plastic bag and give it to a friend - with the express instruction NOT to give it back to you for a set period of time. Or BLOCK HIS number and the number of HIS FRIEND - do this IMMEDIATELY. BLOCK HIS NUMBER ON YOUR HOME PHONE. START WRITING...write it all out. If you can't make your hands move, start talking aloud to yourself - and don't stop. Make sure your son is safe and practice forgetting about the girl, you are going to have to work at it. - PLEASE, every time you think of her tell yourself, 'it isn't about her', SHE IS JUST A PAWN. Say it over and over again, CAUSE IT IS TRUE. About the N: IF HIS

MOUTH IS MOVING or his fingers are texting, HE IS LYING! L-Y-I-N-G!! BREATHE!

Don't forget that any attention – good, bad or indifferent – is attention nonetheless and will serve to as delicious narcissistic supply. This supply gives the N an instant temporary boost *up and out* of his true, tortured self. Because he exists day to day as basically an empty shell of a man, the narcissist is always on the look-out for new sources of supply to jump-start the dead space…to jolt him with a shock of excitement. Don't ever be fooled into thinking that during the calm times, the N isn't still on the prowl and being ridiculously promiscuous – because he is. By his very nature, he feels utterly compelled to ensure that his well of supply never runs dry. This would also explain (but *not* excuse) why a good number of victims harbor a nagging suspicion *during* the relationship that the toxic partner may even be bisexual. I know that *I* did. Most narcissists, although they'll pretend otherwise, actually have no preference either way and can, in fact, swing *both* ways on the fly simply because having sex with anything makes them feel alive! Sure, you and the N might have a fantastic sex life together. For years and years, I thought the same thing. But, guess what? It wasn't real. It was a lie. A narcissist is capable of having terrific sex with anyone that he happens to be fucking. Why? How? *Because that's what he does! It's **all** he does!* (think: scene from *The Terminator*).

Thanks Aileen...thank you so much. You're right about Xmas. My son is twenty but he is a diagnosed schizophrenic and he counts on me. And he deserves better than this freaked out mom although he is my best bud about it because he's been through it ALL with me and the N. He KNOWS what the N is doing and it is only now - after ten years - that he is showing his disdain for the treatment and it has pretty much gotten to the N. Up until now, my son has ALWAYS been kind and caring to the N - without fail - because he wanted it to work to, of course. I remember once the N said to me these telling words: "I've figured that as long as Sky is still nice to me when I come back, I'm good to go". And he knows he does not have that now - sick MF that he is. Since I banged out the LF letter/post earlier, my son and I have had a nice talk and next week we're going out together. One Step.....Thank you, thank you.... My mother...well, she really doesn't want to hear it and I'm not sure she'd understand because even though we've been together ten years, she's met him maybe twice and it wasn't like I flashed him around to my family. I think I've always known that he was what he was - but it wasn't until about 8 months ago - when I discovered LF - that I had the "ah-ha" moment and realized it had all been a farce. It was the worst day of my life. However, I was then able to predict what he did before he even did it. I'd say, "I'm on to you" whenever he'd lie or gaslight or whatever and he'd flip out and storm off. He never even asked **why** I was saying that - the MF knew and he hated it. No, I never admitted to the FB letter. I didn't even mention names but it was very, very obvious who I was and who I was talking about. But, still, I never admitted anything so there's no proof and I've since deactivated the profile and disappeared. Even in my crazy messages to him since, I've acted like I don't know why he's done what he's done. I'll take it to my grave. The girl is what's killing me - even more now than when I knew for sure that he had cheated on me with her. Even though he's ruined every Xmas for nine years (and B'days and all holidays), I still feel jealous that maybe he was with her yesterday and today (planning together my demise) and I hate that yucky feeling. I couldn't eat today - all I wanted to do was sleep.

I will keep repeating "SHE'S A PAWN" until I believe it. I'm crying now as I'm writing this. It still hurts. My girlfriend said, "I know that you feel hurt and all that, but *this is BULLSHIT! He is just evil and has no place in your life! A restraining order on Xmas Eve????? WTF!"*

Keep in mind that sex alone isn't the only thing that feeds the narcissistic monster. The ability to control comes in at a very close second with the ability to manipulate right behind it. Behaviors that constitute "gas lighting" (i.e. making you actually believe that you might be mentally unstable) and the conducting of silent treatments and other degrading and demoralizing punishments are also on the list of perfect spirit-lifting foods for the narcissistic partner. When you find yourself wondering how on earth he could have possibly found yet *another* hurtful boundary to cross, keep in mind that he's starving all the time and a starving person will always come up with creative ways to get nourishment. It really *is* that simple. It's a big part of who he is.

From Henry:

Dear luckyzb, you have only been out of this ten year relationship for three months. You are acting very normal. I think we have all done the yo-yo thing with our emotions. Sometimes we are so strong and so sure we can do this, and then they reappear and our emotions go on auto pilot and we are a mess. These 'episodes' are little lesson's, little reminder's as to why we were on that floor in a fetal position to begin with. It has taken me two years to completely disconnect emotionally from my s-ex. He reappeared recently after two years no-contact and I did not open the door or speak to him. All the same I had a little melt down. I couldn't believe I didn't open that door, because deep down I have wanted him to come back. But I don't want to be in that fetal position or fog ever again and that is all he has to offer me. You know in your heart this guy is bad. Just stop beating yourself up, and go no contact again. And change your numbers - tomorrow. Most phone providers will change numbers with no charge if you tell them you are getting harassing calls. You don't have to explain a thing to them just tell them someone is harassing you. Also when I changed my numbers two years ago it wasn't only to prevent him from calling but to prevent me from waiting on his calls that may or may not come...Cheer up you are doing fine...

Me:

Thank you, Henry. I know how hard that must have been to have him in your space out-of-the-blue. I'm so glad for you. Talk about a test! Kudos! I know it's only been three months. It's not like we'd never had those N break-ups (1000's probably) but this was the first time I went NC and felt good from the get-go. I didn't even cry, I was so mad at him and had simply had enough. I thought there was nothing he could do to get me back in his web. Then, when all he had to do was pull up and say "call me""and I did the backslide - OMG. Then - to top himself with the biggest discard (and quickest) of all, to wreck me instantly and send me on the drive-bys, anxiety, panic, waiting by the phone within hours. It was so deliberate and such a setup - it just makes me want to know why, why, why - and I was SO past all that. I had realized there were no answers, no closure to be found, I had accepted it and I felt alive and happy and everyone noticed. Over the three months, he'd ring the cell here and there just to let me know he was alive, throw rocks at the window in anger, text..I ignored everything. It was only when I started to have my weak moments - after the too-soon dates - that he got the whiff of my weakness and came in for the kill.

Two days until I get the restraining order on him and let the cops serve me with his (bogus) order. Late this evening, four of my girlfriends offered to write statements to send with me to the court to ensure I get my order as quickly as he seems to get his. One of them is taking me down there to make sure I go. After all this bullshit, I still had the urge to drive by his house tonight - but I didn't. And I felt like *ringing his cell two minutes ago. But I didn't. And I thought about writing a letter and getting it out before the order just to have the last word. But I'm too tired. It's 4:00am and I should sleep. But I won't.*

Let me put it this way... if you and the narcissist were stranded on a desert island and it looked as if the food source at some point in the near future was going to run low, he would (literally) eat you. Yup, that's right...he'd kill you and eat you like a cannibal....and *long* before the food supply ran out. He'd have no choice because he always thinks ahead. Moreover, since he has no (nor did he *ever* have) feelings for you, it's all rather easy. In fact, he'd kill you, cook you, and stock up the cave with your barbequed remains so he could survive the cold winter. All without blinking an eye!

Think I'm being harsh? Think again. What's the difference between that scenario and your life with the N right now? To the narcissist, every day is another day stranded on a desert island - and he's out for #1.

Chapter XIII:
Picking His Victims

So, perhaps you're reading this little book and wondering how you happened to get the luck of the draw. Let me ease your mind just a bit by telling you that *it can happen to anyone*. I say this because I still – even after writing two books on the subject and building an *entire website* around the topic of narcissism (thenarcissisticpersonality.com) – *can not* for the life of me come up with a definitive answer as to why we end up in this awful place. I won't say I haven't a clue because *of course* I have clues…I have *lots* of clues…but like everything else that has anything to do with a narcissist, we must always be wary of where fabrication ends and truth begins. How the fuck did I get to a point of no return with a guy I'd known for over ten years prior to our "getting together"? Makes no sense to me. I've never even *come close* to being someone who others might call naïve or gullible. In fact, I'm quite notorious for being the exact opposite – a cynical non-believer of *anything* unless a point is proven. In other words, almost everything is untrue to me until proven otherwise. So what in God's name happened? How did I end up believing all of *his* shit? Considering the fact that I've *yet* to meet or correspond with a victim of narcissist abuse who *isn't* extremely savvy, smart, and beautiful, *how the hell did we **all** get here?* It's like belonging to a secret club where one of the biggest requirements to get in is our willingness to commiserate together at the proverbial emotional toilet bowl while our sanities swirl unfettered down the fucking drain. Holy smokes!

But, seriously now, here's what I *do* know: if our relationship partner is, indeed, a bonafide narcissist, by the time we've realized something sinister is brewing (and we *will*), chances are high that we're already hooked to the drama. It's a ride on the emotional roller coaster from hell and the narcissist is at the controls. We stay because we want to keep the "dream" alive. In my case, I loved the idea of having a soul mate...of building a life together with someone who was already my good friend ....someone I could trust....someone I'd known half of my life. In retrospect, the idea sounds wonderful and I'm not saying that it could never happen. However, when our partner is a narcissist, we're simply never going to change the fact that the idea, as sweet as it sounds, is completely unrealistic.

The truth of the matter is that a narcissist or sociopath *picks us*. Whether we've known them for ten years or ten minutes makes no difference at all. He chooses us because we meet either his current or his future needs. In essence, he sees in us the strengths and weaknesses that will ultimately allow him to benefit from our company. All of our good qualities are mirrored back to us by narcissistic deception so that we see this person as being the best of who we are - our *soul mate*. We are love-bombed into believing the lie. Don't forget, good or bad, this is *why* the N exists on this earth (and that prompts questions for an entirely different book someday). He streamlines our codependency so that he can move along the game board with the least resistance. *He is very good at what he does.*

For many years, I turned the other cheek, addicted to not only the chaos and dysfunctional interaction but also to the sex. I wanted to believe that he couldn't possibly touch anyone else the same way that he touched me. Deep down, I went as far as to think that, even if he did, it would be a fleeting moment and he would return, realizing his mistake. This is exactly why I ended up forgiving him the one indiscretion where I all but caught him red-handed.

There were many more, I am certain, but I never could prove anything. If I couldn't prove it (and it wasn't like I didn't *try* to prove it – I did), then, in the back of my weary mind, the reality of the indiscretion was easily faded.

Good morning everyone - I got up today and came right to the computer. No fetal position but I have those bad butterflies in my stomach. I'm so grateful for all of you - I feel like there are wonderful, friendly ghosts of all of you all around me, hanging out in my room.... And Aileen..I know you are right about the girl. I know how he is ...gets bored with everyone but me very, very quickly. In fact, there's nothing about me that bores him at all and that's one of the reasons he comes back. He's told me that. What's different for him this time is that, when I met with (breaking NC) two weeks ago, I didn't let him come up to the house. That would have been the beginning of something far worse than this.

He was trying to feel me out, probably had a fight with his mom, wanted out, some place to go, wanted to see if he could still just move in and out like before. He has been living here on/off for ten years. When I said no, he had to juggle quickly with whatever he's got going on, started lying, still trying to keep me in the fold. When I outed him (anonymously) to that girl on FB after realizing what he was doing, he became absolutely livid - doing the two things that he KNEW would send me into an anxiety/panic-ridden frenzy: he called my mother and went to file an Order of Bogus Protection. I'm sure he already regrets the order but it's all he had left since he couldn't come up here and create his chaos. And know the girl - if she isn't already gone because of what I wrote - is only the supply because obviously it wasn't going to be that easy to use me and be where he is most comfortable. He will do anything necessary to get whatever he needs at the moment. It's, of course, sad to me that he couldn't be normal, mean all the things he said when we met that night, and TRY to act on his words. This time, more than any other, I am aware of the lack of ACTION in his words. How they will say anything and everything - the same things over and over to appease you - and then do absolutely NOTHING. The words/promises just pour out of their mouths and then they continue on. He was so used to me NOT EXPECTING the "action" - so used to me being happy to just HEAR the words and him not having to ever worry about acting on them. This time I told him that he couldn't come up until I knew he was getting ready to leave his mom's and get his own place, that I could SEE all his plans in progress. He didn't like that. Thinking about that right now makes me sick. Everything after that first meeting and right up until he got the Bogus Order was null and void to him because he already knew that - for the first time in ten years -I had EXPECTATIONS and had set boundaries that were going to be a little harder to cross if he wanted back in. Consequently, he went right for the jugular by calling my mom, filing an Order as if he's IN FEAR FOR HIS LIFE, and, now, the absolute silence.

Nothing, but nothing, has any meaning at all to them. They live twisted moment by twisted moment and time stands absolutely still. I want to scream at him, hit him, ten frigging years and it really was NOTHING. Now, a day and a half until I have to file that Order. That's a really big deal for me because I have never ever done that and he doesn't think I will. I mean, it is such DRAMA. He didn't have to go that far. Sometimes I think I should have let him come up - because it's when he's here, hanging out, invading my space, that I am the strongest and he annoys me the most - to the point that I am GLAD when he leaves. Maybe I should have done that. Maybe I made this so much harder on myself. I should have just let him up to dig his own grave. Maybe I wouldn't be feeling this awful rejection feeling again. This is what's on my mind today.

So, *how* do narcissists determine our worthiness? Rumor has it that a narcissist will choose us because they sense our potential to be co-dependant (and because co-dependants are eager to please those that they love). This makes sense, of course, and the way that the N comes to know that we will serve his purpose is by attentively asking us questions during the Idolize phase and doting on our answers. In my case, the N already knew me and was well aware of my relationships with former boyfriends and how loyal and loving I had been. He also knew, from being a confidant, how my heart could be broken and that I wore that heart on my sleeve. Knowing a whole lot about me ahead of time made the task super easy.

Narcissists also understand that co-dependants have a high tolerance threshold for emotional pain and will put up with being damaged in order to "fix" the other person. To an N, it becomes, in a sense, all about scoping out the person in the room who has the capability for loving unconditionally (a capability that they obviously do not have) and in these types of relationships, this quality is not necessarily going to work towards your benefit.

The main difference between a person who will tolerate the "affections" of a narcissist and someone who won't is a willingness to set boundaries. Co-dependents are typically skittish about setting boundaries of any kind as this indicates the willingness - and an ability - to take control of their own lives. The ability and willingness to set boundaries is a person's only protection against narcissism. Co-dependents love so deeply that they allow their boundaries to be breached over and over. They will tolerate behavior that, prior to this particular relationship, they would have never envisioned themselves tolerating. They will try as hard as they can to prove their love for these monsters over and over, begging and pleading for the same love in return – but, as we know, that never comes. And it never will.

THOUGHT OF SOMETHING FUNNY TO SHARE: Something the N (his name is WAYNE, by the way) said while we were sitting in the car for three hours two weeks ago - that first meeting after NC. It just goes to show how they are nothing but empty words but it's kinda FUNNY. See - for the months prior to me kicking him out, I started saying "I'm on to you!" to everything he did so, when I'd leave, he'd go snooping in my computer and must have come across the "narcissist" stuff/ research/LF I'd saved or whatever. I know this because, at one point, he had gone down to harass one of my girlfriends about me and I guess he blurted out to her "She's nothing but a narcissist!" She thought that was hysterical and I was, like, "ah-ha!" Well, when we sat in the car two weeks ago - and he was "pouring out his heart to me" this was an actual piece of our conversation (shows the mentality of these idiots, I swear). Something to this effect: The N: "I love you and Sky. You were my world. I think about you every minute. I've changed. My life is so different now. I wish I had done more for you guys. I love you" blah blah... Me: "But you hurt me all the time. It's always the same thing. You break my heart" The N: "I know, you're right. I've been a narcissist and I'm so sorry" Me: "Yes, you ARE a narcissist. Do you know what that means? It means you are incapable of love, you have no remorse, no conscience...you'll use anyone and say anything to get what you want. It's awful" The N: "Yup. God, you know me so well. Anyway, I love you, I miss you.........blah blah BLAH BLAH BLAH" True story. Jeeeeez!!!!

From Aileen:

Dear luckyzb, my sociopath told me the exact same thing - that I was the most interesting person he knew, the only one he didn't get bored with! Don't listen to that. It's sociopathtalk. Means nothing at all.

Me:

Eileen........How truly bizarre that all their brains are wired EXACTLY the same...right down to the EXACT same words......the scientific/medical anomaly of that alone is worth studying......frigging amazing

As I stumbled through this period in my life, I spent many hours trying to understand how I had gotten to this point...what made me give the best years of my life to a man that couldn't be loyal to me, not as a partner or even as a friend. Once hostile morning, just a couple of years before the end, I demanded that he *tell* me he was loyal. I wanted to hear the words. He couldn't do it. That day, instead of lying to me, he just stared at me, neither denying nor affirming. He couldn't bring himself to say it either way and the silence was deafening. Although I then, in a flurry of tears, kicked him out, this was just another incident where I would beckon him back or he would return. It was an endless cycle. Just the fact that we were back together after that confirmed for the N that the sky was the limit on what he could get away with. *Wow! Now she pretty much **knows** that I'm not loyal and she **still** took me back. How smart of me to keep my mouth shut!*

Obviously, I can be very co-dependent and that is still, to this day, bizarre to me. I mean, who wants to be thought of as co-dependent? I think we always prefer to see ourselves as simply one of those women (or men) who "love too much" and just happened pick the wrong person. But how does *that* happen? Although this book was not specifically written to address the issue of co-dependency, those of us who've survived this experience certainly must address it at some point lest we repeat the performance with somebody else. Or *would* we? If we'd never behaved like this in any relationship before the narcissist then who's to say that we would ever do it again after the narcissist? These are questions that I recommend we all ask ourselves on the road to recovery. We deserve to be the best that we can be!

As I sit here, I am worried about my own intentions - honestly. Am I hoping that by getting the Order back on him, he'll freak out and contact me again? I HAVE to do it because I can SO imagine him - as soon as I'm served - contacting me, starting a fight, and then calling the cops. Here, in Tucson, even if HE comes here or contacts ME - as long as he's the one who filed the Order, I will be the one who goes to jail. I'm just stressing today that I'm still playing the game - right now, this moment, still....I don't know! I don't want to be...but it is ALL about the small stuff....and I hate that. And I am so mistrusting myself right now as I even write this. I am doubting my own intentions and I am SO hating this!

When you love a narcissist, you become the canvas upon which he projects his internal pain. Partners who love too much make the perfect catalysts for his evil ways......the perfect subjects to abuse and neglect and lie to.

And just a short month or two ago, I wouldn't have played the game if my life depended on it. I can't believe I fell this far back!

The N will choose you because you have a good soul or a stellar reputation or a pocketful of cash or the means to make more of it. He knows he is garbage and will suck your spirit from you as he tries to *become* you. He wants to mirror your goodness and at the same time take it from you.

All he did was pull up and mouth the words "Call me" and - BANG - I leaped right over the edge back into the abyss!

He wants to steal your light – and he will...even if it takes him many, many years. He has all the time in the world to make you suffer because the rest of his time is occupied by other women...other victims that you will never know about. During the course of the relationship, you will be the only one that ever feels lonely. Not the narcissist…ever. No matter what he tells you and no matter what you'd like to believe.

From Susan:

Dear luckyzb, the order of protection that you file against him is so that he cannot come near you and start "something" and you go to jail. EVEN if you are not sure of your intentions right now for getting it, it will protect you if his intentions are bad (and you can be SURE of that) You need to protect yourself if he plans on approaching into your space. See that is what they do. You know his intentions are bad. that is a no brainer. However, he has you struggling with your own. Don't give him that. Think about the arrogance of it all. Him mouthing the words to you "call me". How arrogant is that after months of NC? As if nothing has happened. This is HIS reality but it doesn't have to be yours. The obsessing is the hard part. Try if you can to distract yourself with something else. A little bit at a time. Watch a movie, take a walk, call a friend (and not talk about him). Write down what you need to do on Monday and then try to let it go. For an hour at a time. Then try two hours at a time.

When you do find out about the first "affair", he may admit to *that* one but never to another. Ever. You will make yourself sick thinking that he is treating someone else better than you but he isn't – and that's a fact. He can't love the next victim any more than he can love you and this is because he can't love at all. I realize that this fact offers little comfort in the big picture but you must understand it. Accepting his inability to love at all will save you a load of heartache down the road, I promise you.

From Kathy:

Hi luckyzb, I've been reading your posts, and I feel for you. How frustrated you are, how angry with him, and annoyed with yourself. But here's something that might be good news. Based on what most of us have gone through here, your initial smooth sailing through NC might have been a form of denial. Because really, this guy put you through so much, and maybe you have to deal with some of the hard realities, before you can heal and extricate yourself in a way that is solid and lasting. Okay, so you're mad at yourself. But what is pervasive through your e-mails is an avalanche of insight about his behaviors and processes. Maybe they're not all new for you, but this last experience has really been a major confrontation with not only what he does, but its impact on you. If you didn't really have that straight before, it sounds like you do now. Here's something else that, in my mind, is a good thing. Your anger and resistance is becoming less intellectual and more visceral. (It may have been before, but it doesn't hurt to have another round of flat-out fury with their selfish, manipulative predation on our lives. Just to keep it clear who the bad guy in this scene is.) And here is one you might not agree with, but your out-of-control feelings and behavior that you regret, even your tears and feelings of grief and helpless, are also part of this progress in healing. There's the part of you that hasn't yet de-toxed from him, and the part of you that's going "Oh wow, I really need to take this seriously. If I don't want more of this insanity, I'm going to need to be more careful." I'm not big on beating myself up in order to create self-discipline. I think that we learn our lessons pretty clearly, when it comes to dealing with sociopaths, by the hell we go through when we don't do a good job of taking care of ourselves. You just got a lesson that you won't forget, no matter how much you may miss him until you're fully detoxed. And taking care of ourselves is the number one defense against these characters. Finally, I'm really impressed by watching you process. Sure, you're in an emotionally complicated situation. But you're distilling insight, meaning and new rules for preserving your safety and wellbeing every step of the way. I once read that depression is part of the learning process. When we already know the lesson but we're resisting it. I suspect that the kind of thing you've just been through is something like that. These big "mistakes" and emotional blow-ups are a kind of self-test to see if we've really got it yet. I think you're doing great.

From Denise:

Dear luckyzb, in my journey of ongoing recovery, I can appreciate your struggle. But I also know that finding the missing pieces for self-love and self-respect can help you figure out your next steps. In my research, one thing that stuck out among the information is where a certain author explores a flip side of co-dependency which she refers to as covert narcissism. It rang true for me that, having grown up in a family where as a child I was forced to take on adult responsibilities and do care-taking for people around me, my own normal healthy narcissistic needs were ignored. Co-dependency has similar traits as narcissism when you really examine aspect of this care-taking role, primarily that of a "false self" that is unrealistic -- expected to always be understanding and self-sacrificing and never angry. These and other qualities of co-dependency can add up to a "not-real" person, wouldn't you say? "The codependent person becomes entangled in an over-focus on others (originally on the addicted person)." Payson goes on to say that a primary problem in addressing issues of codependency is difficulty with the inherent issues of "covert narcissism," which often get lost and remain unidentified because they are hidden or invisible to us who were trained to be co-dependent.

We can cut things down to size mentally (through reframing how we overlooked our strengths and saw more strengths in them even with their flaws) and regain perspective. They are humans with flaws just like we are flawed -- albeit in very different ways -- and they do not deserve more concessions (through our empathy and co-dependency caretaking behaviors toward the N) than we give ourselves. So yes, this means we can cut ourselves some slack as we make mistakes and continue to learn and gain strength in understanding more and healing from old wounds. This knowledge provides a foundation to help us become less and less vulnerable to relapse when dealing with addiction to another person. The addiction, when broken down, often has to do with something missing within ourselves -- our own disowned selves. We can reclaim our own positive qualities and stop downplaying our real strengths. In doing so, we will start to believe that we deserve fairness and reciprocity in our relationships, and we will become less tolerant of those who are either incapable or unwilling to meet us half way.

Chapter XIV:
No Contact

I couldn't possibly write a book about loving a narcissist without including a chapter on No Contact (NC). NC, of course, is the only true way to break free from a narcissist and, thus, the only possible and available "cure" for the pain that you feel. That being said, let me make this point: *Understand that all of this - everything you have read on these pages - can happen to you no matter how intelligent, sexy, pretty, wealthy, successful, educated, or intuitive you are. It may be happening to you at this very moment and this is why you are here reading....because you need validation...you need to see the words with your own eyes...the words that describe in exact detail the mental anguish and heartbreak that you are dealing with on a daily basis.* Narcissism is very common and you mustn't feel isolated. It can happen to anyone.

As I stated in the first few sentences of this book, over three million narcissists walk the earth *right now* and they don't exist as only boyfriends and husbands.

Narcissists come disguised as friends, girlfriends, mothers, fathers, sisters, brothers, sons, daughters, bosses, and co-workers. Although implementing NC is more difficult, to be sure, when the narcissistic partner is also the father of your children, it's actually not as difficult as you might think. Why? Because a narcissistic personality does not a good parent make. He will just as soon disappear on the children as he would on you, his partner or wife. No remorse is no remorse no matter who the recipient is. Moreover, any attempts to fight for custody or to endear himself with the children (typically behind your back) is never done out of parental love but only out of spite. There is no boundary that a narcissist will not cross to lessen his own narcissistic injury caused by a divorce or separation. Since complete no contact is obviously impossible when co-parenting, all contact must be kept to a minimum. This means no nasty texting back and forth in between picking up the kids or late night phone calls to either fight or have phone sex. No bickering over the girlfriend or boyfriend. No contact means showing no emotion whatsoever no matter what he says to try and push your buttons. The key is to always show **indifference** and **detachment** at all times. Do not feed into his attempts to get you fired up.

And emotion you show can and will be used against you in or out of a court of law.

For those relationships where marriage and/or children aren't an issue, going NC means exactly what it means – *no contact whatsoever*. Online narcissist recovery blogs such my own (TheNarcissisticPersonality.com), Lovefraud.com, LisaEScott.com, and BaggageReclaim.co.uk are *the* places to visit if you want/need a motivator for maintaining no contact. The women who write for these websites, including myself, are straight-up and will tell you exactly what you have to do. Having never been too good at NC myself, I can tell you that it is terribly hard and emotionally devastating. However, because I tried unsuccessfully to separate using other methods (i.e. remaining friends and/or friends with benefits), I can also tell you that no contact is the *only* way to rid ourselves of these energy suckers. At the same time, it's important to be aware of your *intention* in doing this because, as you remove yourself from the situation, you may find yourself actually using NC as a way to *get him back*. As you try to remove yourself from your situation with NC, you may find yourself actually using NC as a way to *get him back*. When you do this, you are, in essence, just giving him the silent treatment with the intention of getting him to respond to the silence in the same way that you do to his. Sometimes it works and sometimes it doesn't, but you must recognize that you are doing this because, if you are, it means that you are still playing the game. Believe me, he *will* recognize what you are doing and continue to play right along with you, thus keeping the endless cycle repeating forever and ever or at least until he dumps *you* for the final time. Don't forget…this is the master of the silent treatment that you are dealing with and he will play it for all it's worth. The only difference between No Contact and a Silent Treatment is the **intention** of the outcome and no one knows this better than a narcissistic partner. If you find yourself breaking no contact over and over or allowing *him* to do it, you will know that your intention going in was all wrong.

About five years ago, out of the clear blue, I had a burst of empowerment and decided to go no contact on my ex before he had a chance to go silent on me. It was highly unusual behavior on my part and a shocker to both of us since it was he who typically called the communication shots. I was able to hold tight for quite a few weeks until his incessant pounding on my apartment door caused me to open it, letting the evil in once again for another round.

Now, at some point before I gave in, I had scribbled the words "No Contact" on the dry erase board that hung on the wall behind my desk. I had done this as a reminder/affirmation, I suppose, of what I was supposed to be doing. For whatever reason, after I allowed Wayne to come back, I neglected to erase the reminder, deliberately and perhaps purposely, opening myself up to ridicule and arguments as to my intention in initiating the silence. For several weeks, there I sat at my desk in my office and there he sat at his desk across the room and there sat those words – "No Contact" – looming on the wall behind me like the elephant in the room and neither of us said a word.

Then, one day, I happened to turn around to write a date on the board and noticed that the N had made a change – albeit when I wasn't looking - to my scribbled affirmation. With a black marker, he had drawn an angled line through the word "No" in "No Contact" and written "Mo" above it so that it now read "Mo Contact" (as in slang for **More** Contact, of course). I have to admit, I thought it was pretty funny then and I think it's pretty funny even now. I left that "correction" up on that dry erase board for months after and, again, it stared out from the wall behind me and we never said a word. He had obviously been mocking my lame attempt to end the relationship and I knew it. If I hadn't of thought it was funny, I might have had a different reaction but the truth was that he was right. In our relationship, no contact eventually meant *more* contact and that defeats the entire purpose of the strategy!

How can the narcissist take no contact seriously if his victim doesn't? He can't. To a narcissist, there's absolutely no difference between a silent treatment and a little dose of no contact and, hell, he knows *all about* the dynamics of a silent treatment. Specifically, he knows that a silent treatment doesn't last forever and, therefore, the same rule must apply to the No Contact Rule. This is how he thinks when we don't show him differently...when we don't mean what we say and say what we mean.

Most of us *do* understand that implementing no contact is and always will be the only effective means to gaining back our sanity. So, we spend a lot of time talking about it and trying to create new and better ways to maintain it so that we don't do exactly what the narcissist thinks we're going to do – *give in*. It's all about the intention of your strategy. When you make a decision to go NC, you have to ask yourself "Am I going no contact, or am I giving him the silent treatment?" because silent treatments, as we know, are temporary. A silent treatment is typically intended to prove a point or to teach a lesson or, in the narcissist's case, to buy time to be a cheating bastard. The irony of such a punishment is that is clearly a break-up in disguise only the narcissist never says the words – he just disappears leaving you to wonder. It also keeps you in the queue so he can return whenever he's ready. This is the narcissist's intention all along. The intention of The No Contact Rule should be nothing other than to *end it*. Sure, it would be nice if No Contact *hurt* the narcissist but this is doubtful. Narcissistic injury is not the same as the gut-wrenching feeling we get when we're being discarded via a silent treatment. It's not even close. What NC does do, however, is actually give us the last word - finally! NC, whether we know it or not, is the closure from the narcissist we've been looking for.

A look back at this post of mine written just one month ago:
"My point is…slowly but surely, I got stronger without even knowing it…until that final day when I let him go once and for all. My son was in the next room that day and he does this great impression of me calmly yelling out from my room this cocky " Buh-BYE-now!" as the P stormed out on what he didn't know was his very last day in THIS girl's reality!!!!! Every girl with a P - let your heart not be troubled!!! It's your Divine Right to be happy and, I

promise you, that your incredible moment WILL come!"

THAT was ME just over one month ago. I just had to look it up. I was halfway through reading it before I realized it was ME and the post I was looking for. You're all so wonderful, thank you again Aileen, Denise, Henry, Susan, and Kathy.....I know...thank you for the uplifting, encouraging words. My worry - aside from doubting my own intentions - is that I've become a control freak just like him and that I am just continuing the game (even if only within myself). I need to realize that my worry in and of itself is a step forward because at least I am "realizing" the notion and facing it. And, I DO agree, that my NC months were spent mostly in a denial state. I most definitely agree.

Throughout, I was amazed at the fact that I hadn't shed a tear after all the rivers I cried throughout the ten years. I knew something was amiss about that. I didn't think, though, that any backslide I had would be this intense. I was hoping the denial state would have hardened me a little - and it probably did as you say. It just doesn't seem like it today - or this moment - but maybe in the next moment. One moment at a time. And I am going for the Order. My girlfriend is making me stay at her house tomorrow night and she's taking me there first thing Mon. Then, I'll call the sheriff/server on the way out of court so he can meet me at my house with the N's Order. I just want to get it all out of the way before noon. If I could do it today, I would. I just hate that he's making me do the court/legal/drama scenario. He knows how much I hate that. But he also knows that I wouldn't typically participate in taking the game this far - even though he does. He's probably counting on that. Oh - who the hell knows! I wish I could send each of you a big bouquet of flowers today - right now, this minute!

Every response and article I have ever read here is so smart, so well-written, so insightful, so full of clarity for others, so insanely SANE. There is nothing like it anywhere for those recovering from N abuse. This is a very, very special place. (Now I'm crying about THAT. Good God!) I said earlier that I was amazed by the anomaly that is narcissism....how they all say and do the exact same things - the almost paranormal aspect to it all. My son is a diagnosed schizophrenic (I have a story online about our journey together) since the early age of eleven. He suffers from chronic auditory and visual hallucinations and for the past ten years (yup - on TOP/along/during the N saga) my mission has been to learn everything there is to know about the illness/the brain/the origins of consciousness/the mind/evil.

You have to dig deep into your soul if you want to get away. You have to figure out your self-worth and be willing to fight your heart for it. It's not easy but it can be done. You have to figure out why you stay! This is your reality and you can change it. Going NC is the only way just as going cold turkey is often the only way to quit a compulsive act of self-medication. What are you self-medicating from? Save your soul from narcissism before you waste the best years of your life.

Researching the medical and psychological reasons for a person's bad behavior is only relevant, in my opinion, if there is a possibility that a person can change. A narcissist can't change. Ever. As hard as that is to wrap our heads around, it is the fact. This is why your N will return time and time again to torture you. Unless you go NC and stick to it (*even if he leaves you first*), he will constantly be showing up later when he feels the punishment has been enough or whenever his new source of supply isn't behaving. One of the NC recovery sites referred to this specific narcissistic behavior as the N hitting the "reset button" whenever he chooses after a certain period of time is passed. How perfect is that? Think about it. He leaves you in the dust and then, weeks or months later, hits the reset button, showing up at your door and climbing into your bed as if nothing happened. Fully aware of how he's managed down your expectations, he simply "resets" the relationship and picks up where he left off, no explanations needed.

How many times has *that* happened in your situation?

What has always fascinated/freaked me out - and still does - is the fact that The Voices heard by schizophrenics - and even many of the visual hallucinations - are universal from one side of the world to the other. My son hears and sees the same things that schizophrenics all over the universe experience. It is very, very bizarre - and there are hundreds of theories as to how the brain anomaly is created to begin with and why it does what it does. The behavior of the N and the fact that all of us here have experienced the same exact things – the disappearances and /reappearances, the lies, the gas lighting, the very words, actions, lack of actions...Now, I know this is a disorder but, today, I am so aware that this is a DISORDER. Why, then, do I have absolutely NO DESIRE to accept it as such like I accept and want to fix my son's illness? I HATE that the N can't just CHANGE! Or at least REALIZE. I have extreme bitterness - as we all do. I have no "sympathy" whatsoever for his DISORDER but my sympathy for those with mental illness is enormous. Or is that the reason why I stay in the drama - because deep down I think I CAN fix it? Is that why we all stay? Now, I'm getting way out there. But it makes me wonder about the whole damn thing....

Going NC allows you to breathe, to take time for yourself, to cry it out, to write a book, to get angry, to do all those things you can't do when he's manipulating the situation to suit his own purpose. It's very hard and it makes you feel a whole spectrum of emotions…but it must be done. Seriously, for those of us who can't pick up and *leave the country* to escape these motherfuckers, NC is *the only way.*

For me, everything changed that afternoon of October 3rd 2012 when Wayne made that final discarding phone call. Sure, there were a few accusatory texts back and forth over the next day or two but then it all stopped. I never called him again and as far as I know, he never called me. The urges to call him – once so all-consuming - along with any urges to do a drive-by (at that time, he lived just three miles away) had simply stopped. In my mind, I was certain he had both changed his number *and* moved away probably within days of the Discard. I felt confused about the odd sense of calm I felt and remember checking myself mentally several times. Was I simply waiting for him to come knocking? Is that why I felt nothing – because I knew he'd be back? But as time passed and one month grew into two and then three and then the holidays passed without fanfare, I knew that something had shifted. Realizing the undeniable truths about what he could never give to me and my child emotionally had become the end game for me. Finally, after all those years..

Our only other point of contact came by accident in March of this year and I'm glad it happened. You can be as strong as you want to be after it's over but there will always be a "blip" here and there.. a skip in the record… where you find yourself wondering if somewhere out there the narcissist is actually being a nice guy for someone else. Well, I got my answer in a big way.

One afternoon at work, while playing with my phone, I came across upwards of ten unopened text messages from the N leftover from the October discard. With a knot in my stomach, I opened just one and it was as nasty as I imagined it might be. In a teeny moment of rage, I typed two little words – *fuck you* – as a reply and pressed "send, never thinking for a minute that his old number would even be in service five months after the Discard. Sending it, though, was good enough for me because I went about my day and night without giving it a second thought.

Bright and early the next morning, my phone started chiming with text message notifications, one after the other. Even then, I couldn't imagine who was texting me that early and so urgently. And, sure enough, it was the N ...and here is what transpired via text over the next 12 hours:

W: *OMG, I just got your message. I can't believe that you still have hard feelings toward me.*

I didn't respond. I was in shock, I think. Several hours went by and then another text came in:

W: *btw...I've found God, Zari. I've quit drinking and I have a Pastor and a church group. Our mission is to be one with God. It's a beautiful thing...not what you think. I've quit partying and I can't be around any of that anymore.*

I still couldn't respond. He found *God?* Well, isn't that the boundary of all boundaries to cross? What he *found* was a group of church goers in recovery who had no clue who he is and what he'd done and where he'd been. Wayne had found himself the *ultimate clean slate.* I'll be damned. In thirteen years, I *never* heard him say a single thing about church or God or praying or anything. It was his last disgusting resort. And he went there.

W: *Zari...let me help you. You know, this is a great*

church. I was thinking about Sky. He would love it here.

Really? You want to take *my son* – that wonderful person (who has a *very* personal relationship with God) that you basically *neglected* for a decade…*you want to take him to church?*. Now, it was *on*. I texted back.

Me: *You found God, Wayne? Really? I'll tell you why I don't believe that. Because I'm pretty sure God would have wanted you to make amends with us…to say you're sorry for what you put us through..for the years you wasted…for the lies. And by the way, Sky just had a quick chat with God and he doesn't know who the hell you are.*

W: *I'm won't give up on you. Think about coming to church with us. Really. It's a beautiful thing.*

The rest of the night was quiet and melancholy in a bittersweet way. I didn't know what to think. Barbie was with me and she knew what I was feeling. It came down to the fact that he had moved on and – pretending or not – he was making it clear that he was a-okay without us. Just another reminder that, for thirteen years, love was a lie and all that time had been wasted.

Maybe he *had* changed. Was it possible? Could a narcissist really find God and change his evil ways? It was certainly giving me something to think about. And then the morning came and, with a text waiting, I got my answer.

W: *Z* [**I knew then, when he called me "Z", that the N was alive and kicking**]*, you want my mother to die? You want me to kill my mother? That's it, Z. You hacked into my phone for the last time. You're through! We've called the cops and they're on they're way. You're done!*

Me: *Well, now I'm confused. Is this the real Wayne or the church-going Wayne?*

W: *You fucking bitch. We're not playing. You're going to jail.*

Me: *There you are! I knew it was you! So, what's your nonsense today? Blah blah blah*

No response. Then, a little later, I sent one more jab for the road…

Wait a minute! Does this mean you're not taking us to church?

We never had contact again. I understood exactly what happened because, you see, I know who he is. Somewhere during the night and before his last text, he realized, in a panic, that I could - and probably would - expose him for everything he was if he brought me into his new circle. And he was absolutely right.

Chapter XV:
A Deal-Breaker Checklist

Don't "settle" anymore in your life. Don't be afraid to set the boundaries that will ultimately save your life. Life is so precious and loving and a narcissist will kill the best years of your life in the blink of an eye. It's time to create a list of the deal breakers that should forever apply to our romantic relationships. I'll go first by sharing some of my own on the next few pages and undoubtedly you will find many of them familiar. An easy way to get the list started is to create deal-breakers that finish off the following sentence:

I will not, under any circumstances, continue to love or share my time with a partner who:

1. doesn't have "my back" *ever* or at least during the times when he certainly should such as times of danger or crisis or when the reputation of myself or my family is at stake. Even if one of us is angry at the other, having each other's back should always take precedence.

2. … is intolerable of the simplest responsibilities

3. thinks that those who cry over anything are weak yet when it serves his purpose, he may produce a single tear out of just one eye at a time. It's fake..all fake. Those who have no heart *can not* cry. Period.

4. only takes me out on a date or for a drink when he's trying to get back in my good graces

5. makes me question my intuition or my gut feeling even when I know I'm on to something

6. makes me feel compelled to "investigate" new things about his odd behavior each and every time I see him

7. makes me feel compelled to investigate *anything at all* about him

8. disappears for days/weeks for no apparent (or no good) reason and then reappears as if nothing happened or with a ridiculous excuse/story to tell

9. appears to have no problem quitting and/or switching jobs whenever it suits him

10. never assumes responsibility for anything

11. "sides" with others *against me* for any reason or talks behind my back

12. attempts to turn others (mutual friends, his/my family, co-workers, etc.) against me when it suits his purpose

13. treats me one way in bed and another way with his clothes on

14. continually breaks promises to me and/or my children and then acts as if he never made them

15. is disrespectful of my property and personal possessions

16. is annoyed when I ask for even the smallest favor

17. will perform tasks he likes to do and then demand credit for these tasks as if they *were* "favors" even though I never asked for them and, in fact, requested that he do something *else*

18. alienates me from his family or especially from those family members with whom I may have grown close

19. has plenty of stories about exes, referring to them as "psychos" or "psycho bitches" or something similar

20. has no stories *at all* about exes

21. designates (without actually saying it) a "safe house" where you aren't allowed to contact him such as the home of his parents/parent

22. changes his cell phone number for any reason whatsoever

23. goes for any length of time *without* a phone. It is absolutely unacceptable.

24. utters hurtful words (such as "I can take you or leave you" or "Why do you love me? I don't even call you") that suggest he marvels at his own narcissistic neglect

25. cheats on me after acknowledging that we're exclusive as a couple or deliberately causes me to feel "jealous" or insecure over those women that he works with or knows outside of - and even within - the confines of our relationship

26. doesn't appear to have any close friends to speak of OR eventually talks bad about the "friends" that he *does* have OR has far more female "friends" than male OR has a whole set of friends that I've heard about but haven't and probably will never get to meet.

27. likes to boast about his amazing ability to "read people". He's really boasting about how he *picks his victims.*

28. crosses personal boundaries with the specific and obvious intent of embarrassing me, hurting my feelings, and/or ruining my job or reputation

29. crosses a personal boundary *for any reason at all*

30. conveniently disappears around for the holidays or for birthdays or for any momentous or celebratory event.

31. creates random chaos (almost daily) for no reason at all and especially after we've enjoyed some peaceful time together. This typical and nonsensical narcissistic behavior is hurtful and deliberately intended to keep a partner in a heightened state of anxiety 24/7.

32. doesn't support me in anything I do or perhaps supports me in the beginning only to have it become a point of contention later

33. has a private/secret fascination with fetish porn and/or porn that leans toward homosexual behavior. It is simply not my style *at all.*

34. doesn't work or care to work in any way as a team player on our two-man team

35. doesn't love me the way that I love him or even appears to be heading in his direction. No matter what he tells me, I will know.

Be good to yourself. Beware of the narcissist and the evil inside. Watch for the narcissist's many human forms…look for the signs, the red flags, and learn from the mistakes that I've made and have shared with you in this book.

36. If you feel that you may be trapped in an abusive, manipulative, narcissistic relationship, then you probably are and it's time to escape with your life and your soul intact. Life is too short to chase after false love and you deserve only happiness, my friend.

Is it hard to wrap my head around the fact that love was a lie for the best years of my life? That the N never even so much as cared about us? That me and my son were a convenient game, easily disposed of, easily erased? That he could have cared less at any given point over those years if we lived or died? Of course it is. And writing this book has put *me back in it*. The last few days, I've had horrible nightmares about him, scary dreams and sad dreams where I was torn, not knowing what to do. Having to write out his behaviors and his antics…to see it all on paper…right here before me that I was nothing…*ever. That every touch, every caress, every kiss, everything that I ever clung to as being good (and there wasn't much) was a lie. Love was a lie.*

But there are certain undeniable truths…questions you have to ask yourself for which there is only one answer….questions about boundaries, about cooperation and compromise…about entitlements….about making new memories for yourself and for your children…about knowing you could die tomorrow without regretting yesterday…..about whether or not you can say without a doubt that the person you love right now has your back at all times no matter what the circumstance. Can you say it? Without a doubt? If the answer is no, then it's time to release your pain and walk away.

I wish for you everything better than what I had with the N. I wish for you peace and prosperity and I pray for you that an escape is easy.

I wish you safe passage, brothers and sisters, girlfriends and boyfriends….Come back to the sane world narcissist free and with the wind at your backs.

Chapter XVI:
Final Words of Wisdom

From Aileen:

Dear luckyzb - I had the same feelings, hoping my sociopath's sociopathy would go away. Even thinking "he would be such a great guy / it could be such a great relationship if he wasn't a sociopath". But the more I read about sociopaths, the more I analyzed, deciphered, deconstructed his words and actions, the more I came to think that...if you take the sociopath out of my sociopath...there's nothing left!!!! He doesn't "have" a disorder, he IS a disorder. Even the "good" aspects of his personality are feigned, fake, and/or mere instruments that serve no other purpose than the sociopath's sociopathic ambitions and needs.

From Kathy:

Dear luckyzb, you wrote that you have difficulty accepting that the N can't change or at least realize. I think we struggle with facing the fact that their disorder makes them so different from us. We assume that, at some level, they see what we see and feel what we feel. And that, under the right circumstances, they can break through. If they're true NSPs, they can't. They live without so much that we empaths take for granted, and they've developed survival skills and character traits in the absence of empathy or belief in connection or belonging, that their inner worlds are as much like ours as as lizards are like cows. Our difficulty in dealing with this is magnified by the fact that they survive in empath society by observing us, miming us, and taking advantage of the key difference between us -- that we feel for each other. They not only appear to be like us initially, but they appear to be extraordinarily attractive and exactly what we are looking for. This is part of their survival technique. If they can't fit in and fool people into caring about them, they can't survive or thrive in empath society. However, they can't really do what we can do, in terms of building things collaboratively for mutual gain, and they also can't maintain the illusion of being an empath, because it's work for them and they tire. (Imagine trying to pretend you're tough and unfeeling for days on end.)

One of the big challenges we face in coming to terms with them -- and perhaps one of the reasons you're resisting the truth that he's disordered -- is that we naturally feel pity and want to help the ill and disadvantaged. It's not just because we're nice people (we are), but we're conscious of the overall health of the community. Ideally, we want us all to be well, safe and happy. Sociopaths challenge this part of us. Admitting they cannot be healed and, worse, they repay any human feeling with heartless usage and leave behind loss and destruction... well, all this forces us to do damage to ourselves.

We don't want to be as cold and uncaring as them. Most of us have gone through a phase of healing where we're frightened we've become sociopaths as well. It's no coincidence that most of us who get involved with these people don't have very good boundaries or sense of personal entitlement. We are, due to training or result of trauma, "over-socialized" to be communal people. Our understanding of ourselves as separate and entitled to care for ourselves, to get our needs met, and to do this first, before we start sharing our resources, needs to be developed. So, I'm telling you that you can be an empathic, loving and generous person, and still make a personal decision that you are not responsible for other people's problems that you didn't create and you can't fix. In fact, to be a truly open-hearted person, you have to get through first learning to love and care for yourself. That's the path.

Trying to be generous or tolerant or caretaking in any way before you are able to extend all that to yourself, just makes you a walking opportunity for users. The cure to all of this is in your relationship with yourself. To the extent that you're worrying about him or thinking about him or anyone else (except the people who are true resources in your life, like your son), you are avoiding what you really need to be working on. Your relationship with you. Forgive me for sounding preachy. I'm writing fast, because my inner "mom" in reminding me I need to finish cleaning up the kitchen after Christmas dinner and start getting tonight's ready. I hope this makes some kind of sense. Kathy

Me:

I'm not resisting the fact that he's disordered - there is no way for me NOT to accept that in light of what I learned on LF. It's just odd to me that I can be so understanding of mental illness all around (because of my son, etc) and so UNACCEPTING of HIS disorder. It just pisses me off that he HAS one. You are SO RIGHT, though, about what I've been avoiding - things that matter. Eileen - "if you take the sociopath out of my sociopath...there's nothing left!!!! He doesn't "have" a disorder, he IS a disorder."

184

Excellent.....there just isn't any substance to them at all. If you took out the disorder, there'd be nothing but a big, dull void. The disorder just fills up the empty space so they can walk around and pretend to be human.

Me:

And Kathy...you ALWAYS make sense.....and you don't preach - you teach!

From Eileen:

Dear luckyzb: " The disorder just fills up the empty space so they can walk around and pretend to be human" : even better! I agree, it is a terrifying disorder. Schizophrenia, bipolar disorders, and other psychiatric illnesses I suppose, can turn a person into a destructive monster... but we still know there is a person in there! I'd say that's the difference - a sociopath is not a person. We can't help thinking he has a soul, hidden somewhere under layers of compulsive lying, deceiving, cheating, hurting - but there is no soul in there...

Me:

To Eileen...."..psychiatric illnesses, I suppose, can turn a person into a destructive monster... but we still know there is a person in there! I'd say that's the difference - a sociopath is not a person. We can't help thinking he has a soul, hidden somewhere under layers of compulsive lying, deceiving, cheating, hurting - but there is no soul in there..." Thank you for clarifying the difference. This answered my question. I'm embarrassed I didn't think of it like that since my son, who is schizophrenic, is wonderful - so, yes, the lack of SOUL is the difference. Of course it is. The lack of a soul - to me - also defines evil. I'm trying to concentrate on these words right now because I'm thinking about doing something later I shouldn't just to give myself momentary peace. Kathy, I really like the notion of little badges (kinda like the chips in AA) - each a different color maybe to represent how many months NC! That's SO what it feels like - the addiction: "Hi, my name is Zari and I'm addicted to a sociopath..."

Me:

I totally blame him for everything.

Me:

I try to look back and I don't get it. I had a great childhood with loving parents and a terrific college life. Right out of college, I was married to a nice guy for 6 years but we just grew apart and had a very amicable divorce. I guess things got weird then because I immediately left everything I had - great job, great apartment, great friends - and moved from RI to AZ with an Army Pilot after knowing him 3 mos.

Nasty divorce 4 years later but it gave me my son who was very sick from birth (so I was very busy with him). 2nd husband was a complete asshole (still is) but, I have to say, is not what I would call an N/P/S. Had two long-term relationships after that (5 yrs each) and, although I was heart-broken when they ended, I'm great friends with both guys now and neither of them were anywhere close to being an N/P/S. Now, during the very end of my 2nd marriage and during those next two relationships, I knew the N. We hung out together as FRIENDS for almost 12 years. He was in my band on and off but mostly we were friends - NOTHING ELSE (not even a kiss). One fateful night about ten years ago we hooked at a club where I was singing, stayed the night together - shocked because we've always only been friends - and were together ever since.

Red flags were everywhere after about the 2nd week (I remember them) but it was so cool otherwise and it seemed great that we already knew each other so well (Ooops - I obviously didn't!) - so I stayed for ten years until now. You'd think I would have seen it prior to our hooking up...but I was too involved in other relationships to care what the N was doing. I don't even remember who he dated while we were friends. And then, right after we got together, my son had his first schizophrenic episode so that has completely occupied me. I really think I stayed with the N because it was easier than starting over and having the issues with my son to explain to someone new. Plus - I loved him. He was my friend (I thought). Things were very intense back then with doctors and so forth. Then I guess I just got addicted and here I am. So, where do I find a Life Lesson in THAT? Except that I made some very bad choices early on with the N and then chose not to get out of them, the rest of my life before that - divorces and all - seems like butterflies and roses to me right now! :)

Me: *Now that I look at that little biography I just wrote....why the heck did I settle for that idiot way back? I could have had anyone I wanted during the past ten years. The N is NOT all that...Nothing about him was exceptional. I think I was stuck on the length of our "relationship" – a decade. I wanted our "history" to matter - and it hurt that it didn't. I really think I settled because it was the easiest way to deal with my son's crisis and still have somebody in my life. Know what I mean? I think it was Henry who asked once if there was a Life Lesson in any of this....all this suffering at the hands of an N....and my answer would have to be yes, there's always a Life Lesson and I'm sure we're staring it right in the face. Maybe if I knew what it was, I wouldn't be feeling down like I am right now. No matter* *what, though, I am learning a lot. I guess it's like any addiction to a bad thing....we have to take it one day at a time. Well, have a great day, everyone, and, as always, I'm grateful to know each and every one of you...*

Did you enjoy this book? If so, please take moment to submit a review to Amazon! It would be most appreciated.

ALSO, be sure to read the BONUS BOOK EXCERPTS following the ABOUT THE AUTHOR section.

ABOUT THE AUTHOR

Zari Ballard is a home-based Freelance Writer/Author (and single mom!) who resides in sunny Tucson, Arizona at the base of the beautiful Catalina Mountains. In 2005, four years after her son's diagnosis with child-onset schizophrenia, Zari set aside the corporate rat race in lieu of a home-based career as a Freelance Writer. A leap of faith that could have gone either way, the choice was meant-to-be and she has never looked back.

Now, motivated by the popularity of her first four books, Zari intends to devote 2015 and beyond to the world of self-publishing. Her plans include completing a memoir about her son's life, writing a fictional Kindle novel, and creating/recording podcasts about topics in narcissism related to her books. Be sure and stay tuned!

P.S. Zari's been narcissist-free since 10/2012 and plans to keep it that way....:)

Visit Zari's blog **TheNarcissistPersonality.com**

If you enjoyed this book, please do <u>submit a review to Amazon</u>! It would be most appreciated.

BONUS SECTION:
Special Book Excerpt

Stop Spinning, Start Breathing

(Narcissist Abuse Recovery &
the Road to Feeling Normal)

Zari Ballard

Exercise 1b:
Lies, Lies, Lies

I emphasized it in ***When Love Is a Lie*** and I'll emphasize it again right now: narcissists lie even when the truth is a better story. Everything about the relationship itself and as a whole is false…a fabrication….a big fat lie. This habit of the narcissist to lie about everything - no matter what it is or how significant - is the core of our pain…..the nucleus around which our tears revolve day after day after day. My thought is that developing relationship amnesia is just one way our brain protects us from having to obsess about the past even more than we already do. But now….now that we're here trying to recover from the whole mess, we have to focus on all of it, including the lies. Not obsess, but focus. And that's why this section is about putting the relationship in its proper perspective. So, what better way to do that than to talk about all those lies?

How strange that, as soon as the relationship is over, we can't, for the life of us, remember why the narcissist is bad, bad, bad. All we can think about is the great sex or the last time he made us laugh or how long we've been "together" or how cute he is or whatever. Certainly, under normal circumstances, there wouldn't be a problem with thinking back on good times and cherishing certain parts of the relationship. But these are not normal circumstances. The fact is that none of what we remember as being good was ever real. Maybe those moments felt good to us right then but goodness is supposed to last longer than a moment. For the narcissist, nothing – not a single part of it - was real because he/she felt nothing. I know that's hard to wrap your head around but it's the truth.

This exercise is, again, about remembering the relationship as it truly was…the reality of it. While you're hurting, it's so easy to wrap the sadness of the situation in a delusional light but "delusional" is not what we want to be or how we want to feel right now. We want to be clear in our minds about what we just encountered…..the abuse…the manipulation…and, most importantly, the lack of reciprocated love. Unfortunately, we loved someone who was clearly not only unlovable lovable but unworthy as well and we need to accept that and have a clear picture of it. No more relationship amnesia or selective memory.

No more sugarcoating the abuse and offering mental forgiveness before it's due. Now, I know there will be a certain number of readers – just as there were with my first book - who will insist that I don't hold myself accountable for anything. I, of course, know that that is a crock of shit and this isn't about accountability anyway – at least for this moment. It's about betrayal and pain and a broken heart. It's about the butterflies in your gut that never go away and the anxiety, the wondering, and the anger.

In order to heal, we simply must set aside the tears for right now and put the relationship in its proper perspective. Are you ready to begin?

1. *Once, when he disappeared for two weeks...simply vanished...he finally hovered with a text (as usual) saying he had flown back east to visit his sick father for two weeks and had just gotten back. LIE! I insisted that I saw his car around town but he insisted otherwise. LIE! Tickets, please. Nope, he said he'd thrown them out. LIE!*

2. *When he first came back around after being gone for three months and wanted to see me, he was going to come over but called to say his mother had had a stroke and was in the hospital and he couldn't make it. He even faked crying the entire call except he forgot to fake it right*

at the end, letting his voice completely go back to normal right as he hung up and I caught it. A call to every hospital in town confirmed what I knew. LIE!

3. *When he'd moved of his apartment and swore up and down he was homeless and living in his truck. However, when he'd call, I could tell he was in someone's house and even heard voices in the background that he denied were there. It would take him a long to call me back if I left a message. Many other things led me to believe otherwise. LIE!*

Now it's your turn. Looking back, write a few paragraphs, each describing a fictitious story, fabricated excuse, a lie by omission, or just an out and out lie told to you by the Narcissist at any point in your relationship. The lie's level of significance isn't important because a lie is still a lie. Feel free to write out as many as you can remember. Fill up a whole damn notebook if you like. This is a time to purge no matter how painful the memory.

This – the endless lying – is at the heart of the emotional suffering that we endured and that is a fact. To expect us to "just get over it" is not only ludicrous, it's completely unrealistic. Being lied to over and over and over by someone we love is the ultimate betrayal and breeds general mistrust all around. The affects of the narcissist's lies spill into other areas of our lives and disrupt the normal flow of everyday life. It affects our children and our families. Without a doubt, I feel that this is the most damaging part of the narcissist's pathological relationship agenda and the more we purge...the more we accept and release the words of the betrayal, the lighter our hearts will be.

Exercise 1c:
Navigating Cognitive Dissonance

By most definitions, cognitive dissonance is the psychological discomfort or torment a person feels when he or she holds conflicting beliefs about something simultaneously. On other words, we are torn between believing what we want to believe and accepting what we know to be the truth about someone or something. It happens to everyone numerous times in a lifetime and oftentimes will result in our making an important decision that ultimately works in our best interest or for the best interest of our family.

Cognitive dissonance is not always a bad thing because it helps us weigh both sides of a situation and make (hopefully) the best choice based on the truth and on the facts. Cognitive dissonance is not always a bad thing, that is, until it becomes the catalyst for our inability to leave a narcissistic partner or to remain in a state of "no contact" or to not give in to the hovering or to recover from the whole ordeal when it is finally is really truly over. It becomes a problem when it keeps us shackled to a codependency to hope that will never get us anywhere as long as we choose to remain chained.

The hardest part about letting go of the narcissist is our reluctance to accept what we already know to be true – that nothing about anything we experienced in our own mind was real…..that he didn't love us (never did and never will)….that every precious moment, every kiss and caress…all those times when we really thought it was coming around and oh-how-glad-we-were-that-we-stuck-it-out….that all those times were LIES. It was all fake, a fabrication created by the **narcissist** to benefit the narcissist. All those things that we miss – the sayings, the gestures, the witty comments – were falsities….clever workings of a con artist who knew how to present his stuff in a way that tugged at our heartstrings. So, not only do we suffer relationship amnesia when it's over, we suffer selective relationship amnesia, remembering only the best of the best in high definition and with all the sounds and smells in tact as well. No doubt, cognitive dissonance is a bad trick the brain plays on those already suffering the grief of love lost. And, yes, it is very sad.

The fact, unfortunately, is that the narcissist hates you, me, and anyone who truly has a heart. He hates us because we are capable of loving. He has hated us from the day we became his target. Oh, but that wasn't true the *whole* time, was it? Yup, it was. Just think about it. While you may not want to believe it, how many times did he climb out of your bed early after great sex, giving some illogical excuse for the departure and disappear for two unexplainable days …just vanishing into thin air? You get my point. In fact, the N probably did that or something similar to you many times over the years. And what about the sex? Ohhh yes, *the sex*. For me, *the sex* was my *everything*. How could he not love me if the sex was so great? That just wasn't possible! So, okay, he does a million bad things that scream hatred towards me but I'm going to cling to the sex and pretend that *that's* how he *really* feels. Sure, that makes sense. Or does it? And so it goes….our cognitive dissonance sends us to hell and back once again. Struggling to accept that your entire relationship was a fake even though you know in your heart of hearts that it was….wanting to believe that the narcissist must have loved you at some point in the relationship even though you know that no one who loved you would have *ever* done the things that he did to you (and behind your back).

The one belief that saved me from dying from a broken heart throughout my 13-years with a narcissist motherfucker is my belief that all things have to be, for the most part, logical in order to be true. In other words, something has to make sense before I believe it. Towards the end of my relationship, when I couldn't take it anymore...the constant lying and the constant insult to my intelligence, I started tossing out the same response to his word salad: "I'm sorry, but that's not logical, Wayne. It couldn't have happened that way. You're lying" and it absolutely infuriated him. And since he had no intention of ever telling me the truth, he simply started mocking me about it – "Logical, logical, logical...I'm sick of your "logical" bullshit!" and he'd mock me all the way out the door and then, of course, he'd vanish.

You can't argue with logic. You just can't. I used logic to navigate my way through – and up and out of – the muddy waters of cognitive dissonance. And you can too, my friends. In order to wake from a narcissistic nightmare, you must start observing the processes of your recovery logically. Things that make sense are good for you and the narcissist, as we know, is completely nonsensical. We can't keep postponing our recovery based on conflicting beliefs about the narcissist – especially when we know the truth. Unlike a narcissist, we know right from wrong.

To escape the grief and emotional torment of

cognitive dissonance, you have to choose between the two beliefs and using logic is one way to ensure that you make the right choice…..for yourself, for your children, for your future, and for your sanity.

This exercise is about recognizing your level of cognitive dissonance and understanding that there really is a name for all those conflicted feelings…..and I'll go first:

Even though I know now it wasn't real, I still miss the way he'd hold my face in his hands when he kissed me.

Even though I know now he didn't mean it, I still liked it when he told me that he thought I was a really smart person.

Even though I know now it would have never happened, I still wish we could have grown old together like he always said he was sure would happen.

Even though I know now it was just a ploy, I still laugh when I think about how he would "affectionately" mimic some of my more dramatic mannerisms.

Even though I know he could care less about me, I can't help but hold on to the belief that surely he must think of me and my son many times in a day.

Even though he'd done it to me a thousand times and I have absolutely no reason to believe that the next time would be any different, I can't help but think that maybe he really has changed and finally he can stop with this bad behavior, realize what a good catch I am, and love me like I deserve to be loved.

In the section below, I've started a few sentences that you can finish in any way that you want. You'll notice that I start each sentence under the premise that you *already know* that the things that you miss about the N are a falsehood. I've also provided some blank areas as well where you can develop similar sentences on your own based on the pieces of your own experience Again, writing things down – even though it can be bittersweet – is a great way to release the mental image of the lie itself and, so, with this exercise, we'll deliberately allow ourselves a few more nostalgic moments. To navigate the waters of cognitive dissonance, we have to resolve to the fact that whatever we thought was real in the relationship never was. When love is a lie, we simply have no choice but to make the right choice lest we sentence ourselves to waste what's left of our life as well. And be proud of yourself in the process because it's a monumental step in starting over.

Even though I know now it wasn't real, I still

miss:

_____

_____

_____

Even though I know now his feelings weren't genuine, I still liked it when:

_____

_____

_____

Now feel free to make up your own sentences representing the cognitive dissonance you feel about your relationships – the untruths that you can't let go of....the "wishes" for things that you know in your heart wouldn't have or will not ever happen. It is our understanding of the difference that gives us the strength to let go of a relationship that, for all intents and purposes, existed in our imagination. When we finally "get" this, then and only then can we being to break our codependency to hope and, consequently, our attachment to the narcissist.

_____

_____

_____

To begin recovery, we have to decompress and deprogram ourselves from the brainwashing of narcissism. We have to learn to make the right choices and to come to terms with our conflicting beliefs about the person that is hurting us. Once we do that, things start to calm down. Being confused about our feelings…knowing one thing to be true yet *feeling* something totally different is exhausting and will wear your moral, self-esteem, and overall self worth into the ground before you even know what's happening.

Keep an eye on your cognitive dissonance because, if the problem is a narcissist, I am certain you've been struggling with it. Keep your beliefs about this person in check at all times and you will start to see the forest for the trees. Things will go from dark to light and the narcissistic fog he has placed over your life will slowly start to lift. Being mindful of *you* at all times is the only real way of working through the pain.

Exercise 2a:
Why So Much Pain?

Before we pull ourselves up and start working through the pain, we have to understand why there is *so* much pain. Why this relationship is different than *allllllllllll* the others…different than the boyfriends of years back who you could have sworn devastated you (did they?)…different from the husband you divorced even though the divorce itself dragged you through the mud (did it?)…why, why is there *now,* when facing the bright possibility of a future narcissist-free, *so* much gut-wrenching pain…*so* much separation anxiety? Why is it so damn difficult to just suck it up like a big girl (or boy) and *get on* with it? Are we really *that* pathetic? Why *are* we whining? Is a relationship break-up with a narcissist *that* different? Yup, you bet it is.

Oddly enough, most women and men who end up in a relationship predicament with a narcissistic partner are amazed (and disappointed) to find themselves behaving in ways that are completely out of character. It's as if the narcissist molds and shapes the persona of us that he meets (and targets) into lots of little weaker versions that, in the end, don't even resemble who we once were. We are transformed, seemingly in seconds, from confident, successful women and men into needy, whiny newborns...newborns that will eventually be abandoned not once, not twice, but *many* times over before the end comes. And in the end, we *feel* like rejected newborns because whether it ends because he never returns or because we've decided that enough is enough, we still have to start over going forward and I mean *start over.* Suddenly, it's as if the narcissist was the only person we ever loved or who ever loved us and we *know* this isn't true...yet we turn this terrible "mis-belief", this utter fabrication.. into our catalyst for grieving. Lord Almighty, how did we get here?

First, all relationships end "sadly" for one reason or another. Sometimes the sadness is bittersweet which means that both parties love each other but have accepted the fact that, in the best interest of both, it all must end. Bittersweet sadness is what makes a tear-jerker movie a tear-jerker. Bittersweet sadness is what makes you leave the theatre rooting for *both* characters. So, no, breaking-up with the narcissist (a.k.a The Evil One) doesn't constitute bittersweet.

Other categories for break-up sadness might be anger sadness, cheating/infidelity sadness, realized-we're-better-as-friends sadness, grew-out-of-each-other sadness...or whatever. The point is that any of these sadness categories (yes, even the cheating/infidelity), while certainly justification for a break-up, has the potential to heal over time. Face it, there are simply some exes that don't deserve being hated forever – and this goes for you as well, in reverse. Time passes and we get over the hurt without even knowing it. Then, somewhere, someday, you'll see this person and realize that your first reaction isn't a jolt, or an urge to run, or bad butterflies in your stomach. You'll be able to give this person a hug, meet the new girlfriend or boyfriend, chat about the weather or even old times for a minute, and then be on your way feeling perfectly fine.

Now, understand that, with the narcissist, it will never be any of the above – ever. And you *know* it. And *that* is the difference. *That* is why there is so much pain right now and that is why we feel the need to *recover* from the whole damn mess.

A break-up with a narcissist hurts because: 1) you loved him and you thought he loved you, 2) you loved him and found out he *never* loved you, 3) you loved him and found out he'd been with others the whole time, 4) you based your entire future on this false love (and he went along with it), 5) you forgave him for *everything* in hopes he'd see the error of his ways but that never happened, 6) you invested so much time – maybe *years* – for nothing and he offers no apology (in fact, he *blames* you for all of it, 7) his ability to erase you (and even the children, if you have any together) is still, to this day, hard to fathom, and 8) he's simply fucking evil ....*the list could go on and on.*

It's important that you understand that *you* deserve to hurt. You are *not* being a baby, you are *not* being weak, and you are *not* losing your mind. Don't worry about what others think because anybody who judges your pain obviously has *never experienced* this type of relationship *ever* so who cares what they think! And anybody who has experienced it will know *exactly* why you suffer and it's all okay. So, for this exercise, make a list of the elements of this break-up that make it different for you than all the others. Why do *you* think that the pain is so much harder to bear?

_____

_____

My point with this particular section is to let you know *that it's not your fault.* Toxic people are very good at what they do. When others don't understand why we have such a hard time letting go, it's because they don't understand the level of betrayal that's involved in these types of relationships. Much of the abuse is passive-aggressive and passive-aggressive abuse is all about control. It's hard to explain passive-aggressive manipulation because much of it is unspoken and takes place over a long period of time. In one of the reader reviews written for *When Love Is a Lie,* a woman wrote "wow, you've just described the relationship I've been in for 43 years". Forty-three years!! I almost fell off my chair. It made me want to cry, it really did. Can you imagine going through this bullshit for forty-three years? Either can I. But, obviously, the possibility is there.

In the next exercise, I'm going to explain how to appreciate the silence of the narcissist's absence in the wake of a silent treatment or break-up. It took me years to realize the importance of using that time wisely and, when I did, it saved my life and my sanity. If any of you have read self-help books that talk about mindfulness and meditation, silence appreciation is very close to that.

Exercise 2b:
Silence Appreciation

As we talked about in the last section, the N/S/P creates so much havoc and chaos that we become immune to – and codependent upon - the constant din of the narcissistic nonsense. The noise that he creates, of course, is nothing but a distraction – a play of smoke & mirrors – to divert your attention away from what *he* knows *you* know about what he's really up to. Again, it's all in the strategy guide for the pathological relationship agenda and the narcissist follows it to a tee. He makes your world so frigging noisy that you can't possibly pay attention to *every* suspicious behavior (although you try!) or you'd make yourself crazier than you already are. The narcissist counts on this to happen and so he ramps up the volume with nonsense and bullshit and illogical lies until all you hear is the drone of the Charlie Brown "WUA WUA's" every time he opens his mouth. Then, while the noise and chaos is swirling all around you, he disappears or pulls a silent treatment because he's now free to go – at least temporarily – and, although you'll be suffering as intended – you will have been too distracted to really have connected with his malevolent scheme.

My initiation into the narcissistic world of silent treatments was a prime example of a narcissist's determination to get the pain just right. For Wayne, at least initially, it was a bumbling disaster because I honestly didn't get it. *A silent treatment? What's a silent treatment?* I swear to you…I didn't know what that was. I'd never experienced that with *anybody*, rarely even heard about it, and certainly never *expected* it. Consequently, the first two times that he tried to implement it, my unassuming reaction was to leave worried notes and voice mails showing nothing but genuine concern for his health and safety. I thought surely he must be *dead* to be gone so long. This, of course, completely thwarted his plans, forcing him to resort to Plan B which involved making up a quick story, returning quietly to the fold, and committing himself to getting better results the next time around. *Damn it, this isn't working. Doesn't the stupid bitch know I'm giving her the silent treatment?*

Since the whole point of a silent treatment is to obviously be silent, I can only imagine his frustration when, by the second week, he realized that I had no clue he was trying to hurt me. At that point, his only option was to settle in, kick up some more chaos, and crank up the narcissistic noise.

I hope you've enjoyed this excerpt from my book *Stop Spinning, Start Breathing*. The full version is available from Amazon.com in digital download and also in paperback. com.

22952148R00129

Made in the USA
San Bernardino, CA
28 July 2015